CANAL WALKS

CANAL WALKS

Roger W. Squires
photographs by Gareth Lovett Jones

HUTCHINSON
London Melbourne Sydney Auckland Johannesburg

Hutchinson & Co. (Publishers) Ltd

An imprint of the Hutchinson Publishing Group

17–21 Conway Street, London W1P 6JD

Hutchinson Publishing Group (Australia) Pty Ltd
16–22 Church Street, Hawthorn, Melbourne, Victoria 3122

Hutchinson Group (N Z) Ltd
32–34 View Road, P O Box 40–086, Glenfield, Auckland 10

Hutchinson Group (S A) Pty Ltd
P O Box 337, Bergvlei 2012, South Africa

First published 1985

Set in Caledonia by Jolly & Barber Ltd, Rugby, Warwickshire

Printed by Jolly & Barber Ltd, Rugby, Warwickshire
and bound by Anchor Brendon Ltd, Tiptree, Essex

British Library Cataloguing in Publication Data
Squires, Roger W.
Canal Walks.
1. Canals – England – Guide-books
2. England – Description and Travel – 1971 – Guide-books
I. Title II. Jones, Gareth Lovett
914.2′04858 DA632

ISBN 0 09 159590 8

The authors and publisher remind walkers that they should obtain permission from the owner before entering any private property or traversing private land. All the walks detailed in the book are open to the public, but those on British Waterways Board land must be 'taken as they are found'.

FRONTISPIECE *The Grand Western Canal, near Tiverton*

Contents

Acknowledgements

First we must express our thanks to those numerous unnamed people whom we have met on our travels around the English canals, and who were willing to stop and recount their own experiences and provide vital local knowledge that could not be gleaned in any other way. In much the same way the various canal societies have provided detailed information about their canals, and we are grateful to them all.

No one embarking on a study of canals can afford to miss the standard histories by Charles Hadfield. Much of the basic historical detail in this book is derived from this source, although it is often supplemented by other titles mentioned in the text. The authors acknowledge with thanks their use of this material.

Thanks also go to the staff of the British Waterways Board for their courteous help, and especially to Graham Avory, the senior press officer. We are similarly grateful to the Water Space Amenity Commission for their permission to use the maps that appeared in their Research Report No. 1, 'The Potential of Towpaths as Waterside Footpaths'.

Thanks also go to Mrs Doris Wilson and Mrs Sandra Bird for typing the manuscript and to Mrs Amanda Squires for all her efforts in making the preparation of the book run so smoothly.

Restoration of a badly eroded section of a towpath on the Llangollen branch of the Shropshire Union Canal to the east of Ellesmere. Without labours such as these . . .

Introduction

Inland waterways create a variety of pictures in people's minds. Some people see them as a convenient rubbish dump; a watery grave for old prams and mattresses. On the other hand, industrialists look upon canals as a cheap water supply and city firemen regard them as an efficient insurance against small low-pressure water mains.

Today a growing band of people regard the inland waterways as a prime leisure resource. Mile after mile of canal bank is leased to local fishing clubs and increasing numbers of people are taking holidays in hired boats each year, using canals as a chance to get away and take life at a steady pace.

Often, those who are attracted to such holidays have an idyllic image in their minds of painted boats, neat lock cottages and quaint overbridges. They may not realize that the canals were built as arteries of trade to link quarries and works to wharfs, villages and towns. Just as the modern motorways are the current means of moving heavy goods, so canals were vital to trade and industry when they were built between 150 and 200 years ago. Today it is difficult to imagine why such winding routes were selected, or what convinced local promoters to build a wide-gauge canal in a country area, yet only a narrow canal within a busy town. To begin to understand why they were constructed in the way they were we need to study their features at close quarters. That is the virtue of walking the canals: one can stop and admire the views, always so varied in Britain, and study at leisure the designs of the canals which provide such a unique part of our heritage.

Before going out to walk the canals, it is worth knowing something of the times in which they were built. The mid-eighteenth century marked the beginning of the era that we call the Industrial Revolution. Inventions combined with different ways of organizing labour to maximize output. Factories and mills were using new power sources and encouraging people to leave the land and find work in the expanding towns. Better ways were sought to transport both food and raw materials to their new works and to distribute the finished products; old packhorse routes still survived from the Middle Ages, but the winter rains reduced the unmetalled roads to quagmires.

The economies of water transport had been known from the earliest times. Rivers, although unreliable in periods of drought and flood, had provided the means for great cities such as London, York and Norwich to develop and expand. The problem was that the major rivers went nowhere near the new inland coalfields in the Birmingham area or north-west of Manchester. Also the great rivers were isolated from each other, their only link being perilous and potentially costly voyages around the coast.

In Europe canals had been known particularly from the 1550s, when the Dukes of Milan used an inland waterway network to service their town. In the 1660s the Canal du Midi in the South of France was built to link the Mediterranean with the Bay of Biscay and began to prove its worth. Yet in England, the idea was very slowly adopted. It was only after one man's canal in England proved successful, some seventy years later, that other canal builders were persuaded to follow suit. The entrepreneur was Francis Egerton, third Duke of Bridgewater. His canal solved three problems in one go: firstly it enabled him to drain his mines; secondly, it provided a direct route to the centre of Manchester, some 13 miles away, and thirdly the barges enabled the coal from the mines to be conveyed to Manchester cheaply and reliably. Soon the Duke's consultant, James Brindley, was called upon to devise schemes to link the Trent with the Mersey, and the Thames with the Severn, together with a multitude of other routes.

Canals were not national enterprises – invariably they were small schemes developed by single individuals or local companies, often with limited budgets, to meet local needs. However, compulsory purchase rights were needed to procure a path for canals, and the proprietors had to gain an Act of Parliament to empower them to create their new transport routes. Opposition came in various forms: from those who simply did not want the canal near their estates, from old navigation companies who feared rival trade, and even from millowners, concerned with the potential loss of their water supplies. These problems often resulted in deviations, or the provision of special landscaping and ornate bridges, and the free carriage of certain goods for local use. In consequence the outlandish or extraordinary can be found in the most unexpected of places.

The routes used by the various canals were often a compromise, but invariably bear the mark of their chief engineer. Certainly, it has been said of James Brindley that he wrote his signature on the landscape of Britain. Brindley was one of the leading hydraulic engineers; he could apparently work out the path of a canal route by just riding through the area. He believed that canals should be kept to one level for as long as possible, following the contours of the land. His canals therefore go round hills and meander along river valleys. Only when he was forced to change levels did he build locks, and then he tended to group them in flights. His locks, with the 71 feet by 7 feet standard, set the pattern for canals elsewhere. The standard ultimately led to the demise of the canals, in fact, because such small locks restricted the carrying capacity of craft to 25 or 30 tons.

The 'navvies' (short for 'navigators'), employed by local contractors, used simple tools – picks, shovels and wheelbarrows – to carve the canals from the countryside. It is incredible that they achieved such fast results; contemporary records suggest that the disruption caused was no less than that caused by the construction of the modern motorways.

In much the same way as new motorways have supplanted older roads, so a second generation of canal building provided more direct and efficient canal routes. Perhaps the best known of the new group of engineers was Thomas Telford, who perfected the 'cut and fill' technique: digging deep into the higher ground and using the excavated soil to create embankments across the valley beyond. Canals thus became more direct and some of the meandering courses of the earlier canals were straightened and bottlenecks removed. Some of the best examples of such changes are found on the Northern Oxford Canal and on the New Main Line of the Birmingham Canal Navigations.

One of the most spectacular developments in the history of the canals came through the substitution of cast iron for stone in aqueducts, bridges and other structures. The prefabricated sections of cast iron enabled bridges to be built in a quarter of the time, and the cast-iron trough proved a godsend in the construction of aqueducts. There is no doubt that the Pontcysyllte Aqueduct built across the Dee Valley by Telford and Jessop is the greatest single work of the age. It shows how fast canal

TRIAD II

The Market Harborough Arm, near Stone House

engineering techniques had developed in the preceding fifty years.

One of the best tributes to the qualities of cast and wrought iron is the impressive boat lift at Anderton. Built in 1875 by Edward Leader Williams, it used hydraulic power to raise and lower boats the 50 feet between the Weaver Navigation and the Trent and Mersey Canal. On a less impressive scale my favourite construction is the Engine Arm Aqueduct, designed by Telford, which spans the New Main Line at Smethwick on the Birmingham Canal Navigations. Though for sheer simplicity and elegance the Stretton Aqueduct, carrying the Shropshire Union Canal over Telford's Holyhead road (A5), is hard to beat.

Clearly the most lasting elements of the second generation of canals were the dynamic design styles adopted by the later canal engineers. John Rennie, who built the Kennet and Avon Canal, inspired the elegant masonry work of such structures as the Dundas Aqueduct on the Kennet and Avon or the longer Lune Aqueduct on the Lancaster Canal. Even the smaller bridges and the ornate tunnel mouths have distinctive designs. The canals had come of age.

By 1830 most of the second generation of canals had been completed, and at that time there were over 4000 miles of navigable waterways. Brindley's Grand Cross had united the four great rivers of the land and the long Oxford Canal link to the Thames had been bypassed by the new Grand Junction Canal, which offered a shorter and more direct route from London and the Thames to the heart of the Black Country. Such major carriage firms as Pickford's started their business on the canals, ultimately running scheduled services on stage boats and fly boats. The former carried heavy goods, stopping overnight, while the latter were the express services that used relays of horses and men, in shifts, working both day and night. Most canal traffic, however, was local trade. A few craft were owned privately, though most were the property of companies. The boats were carefully painted and maintained.

Later canals such as the Caledonian and the Manchester Ship Canal were of grand design, but by then the railways already had begun to encroach into canal trade. This competition was to have serious consequences for those who worked the canals. In some cases the railway companies bought out the canals; in others they laid their tracks alongside canal lines and syphoned away the traffic. The competition brought cost cutting, which in turn led to a cycle of decline, as lack of investment resulted in lower standards of maintenance and unreliable routes. Canal families were forced to live on their boats when they could no longer afford a land base. Gradually poverty forced even the most loyal of them to seek work elsewhere.

George Smith of Coalville (1831–95), an ardent campaigner for human rights, published *Our Canal Population* in 1875; it set out to bring to the notice of reformers the appalling conditions in which some men, women and children spent their lives afloat in the mid-nineteenth century. One can only do justice to what he saw by quoting from his own account:

> The boat system of inland navigation has gone on increasing year by year until, at the present time, it presents one complete network. . . . On its surface are over 25,000 boats, carrying human beings of all ages, together with filth, mud, manure and refuse of our large towns. Some of the cabins are models of neatness, and a man and two youths might pass a few nights in such very comfortably. Others are the most filthy holes imaginable; what with bugs and other vermin creeping up the sides, stinking mud finding its way through the old leaky joints at the end of the bottom of the cabin, and being heated by a hot stove, stenches arise therefrom enough to make a dog sick.

Our concern, however, is not with the past, but with the nature of canals today. For the most part the structures have remained untouched for the past 150 years. Their history is reflected in the bridges and buildings visible today. Traditional construction methods, together with local materials, emphasize the flavour of the area through which the canals were built. The Midland canals are based on mellow red brick, while further south local grey stone was used for the Oxford Canal near Thrupp. Bridges and locks often became focal points for local trade, so canal wharfs and warehouses were built. Boaters needed rest and their horses needed shelter; as a result canalside pubs with stables were created along the line. Where villages were bypassed, self-contained wharf settlements grew up. In some instances complete new towns were created, the most notable of which is Stourport, where the Staffordshire and Worcestershire Canal joins the River Severn. In other places, inland interchange ports were created where the natural and artificial navigations met. Splendid warehouses and docks – many still visible today – were built at some sites. One of the most remarkable of these, still standing, is at Shardlow, at the junction of the Trent and Mersey Canal and the River Trent. Elsewhere maintenance yards were created to service the canals. One of the most ornate buildings of this type is the Italianate former water tower at Bulbourne Maintenance Yard on the Grand Union Canal at Tring, but my favourite is the group of slate-roofed red-brick waterside buildings at Hartshill on the Coventry Canal.

The towpath bridges are fascinating – a great variety of designs was developed to transfer the towpath from one side of the canal to the other. Special 'turnover' bridges were evolved to accommodate the towrope. The simplest designs were like ordinary bridges but with long approach ramps, so that the horse could walk up the ramp and pass over the bridge, turning back down the ramp the other side, then doubling back under the bridge and continuing, without the towrope needing to be unhitched. Eventually, the more sophisticated 'snake bridges' evolved. The idea was the same but, instead of the long, straight ramps, one ramp curls right round on itself to pass beneath the arch. The best example can be found on the Macclesfield Canal at Marple, Cheshire, near its junction with the Peak Forest Canal. In other cases, cheaper solutions were found: the neatest are the 'split' bridges on the Stratford-on-Avon Canal, where the metal bridges are in two sections, cantilevered out from the canal side, not linking at the centre so the gap allows the towrope to pass through. The bridges themselves often show the signs of past traffic, in the multitude of grooves cut deep into the brick, stone or metal, scored out by countless towropes.

The most interesting of all the bridges are the aqueducts, designed to carry the canals over roads, rivers or even other canals. The very early aqueducts are dumpy structures: their heavy construction relates to the considerable problems the early engineers experienced in containing the hydraulic pressures involved. An example is Brindley's design over the River Sow, near Great Heywood, on the Staffordshire and Worcestershire Canal. Later engineers were able to build on finer lines, using developing techniques. The masterpiece of Benjamin Outram, across the Goyt valley at Marple, illustrates the improvement: here pierced apertures in the arch abutments reduce the dead weight bearing down on the piers.

Much of the canal system was nationalized in 1948. The

notable exceptions were the Manchester Ship Canal, the Rochdale Canal, the Bridgewater Canal, and some abandoned navigations such as the Basingstoke Canal and the Thames and Severn Canal. The Transport Act of 1968 classified the nationalized waterways into three groups: the Commercial (roughly a fifth), the Cruising (just over half) and the Remainder, a number of which were derelict already. The British Waterways Board was given the task of developing each of the groups, according to defined principles, and empowered to negotiate with local authorities to seek funds to revive the Remainder canals for leisure use. Some structures were also designated as Ancient Monuments, which enabled other funds to be tapped for their restoration. Elsewhere, stretches of canal were designated as conservation areas. Local authorities were given the opportunity to adopt some of the towpaths as public walks, especially through towns, provided suitable maintenance agreements could be reached.

Walkers received a boost in 1978 when the British Waterways Board declared the majority of its towpaths open to general public use, but the Board absolved itself of legal liability to maintain the paths and avoided any chance of legal action over unexpected hazards that might be encountered. Since the Board's action, some of the few private canal companies have released the controls on the use of their towpaths as well – although it is still not feasible to walk such waterways as the Manchester Ship Canal, where no towpath exists. It is sensible to check access facilities before contemplating an uncharted walk.

Shortage of cash over the years has meant that only essential maintenance work has been undertaken. As the horse-drawn boats were replaced by motor boats many of the rural towpaths became unused, while those in towns were sometimes barred to stop vandals from damaging adjacent property. In addition, the wash from motor boats has damaged the canal banks where once the towpaths stood. As a result there are several nominal towpaths where it is impossible to walk from end to end. An example is the summit level of the popular southern section of the Oxford Canal, where long stretches between Fenny Compton and Claydon Top Lock have just disappeared into the canal. Fortunately, many towpaths remain intact. Even with these walks, however, a damp spring and a mild summer can encourage excessive undergrowth, which can nearly block the path. For this reason, many

The link channel between the Stratford-upon-Avon Canal and the Grand Union Canal

of the walks identified in the book can be split into sections so that the most visual reaches of the canal can be studied, whilst the difficult or lengthy sections can be by-passed by those who are short of time.

Many local authorities and public bodies are now opening up and clearing their canal towpaths. In Greater London a canal walkway now extends from Limehouse in the east to Uxbridge in the west, with a link to the Thames at Brentford. From Brentford the Ramblers' Association are actively trying to reopen a Thames-side walk all the way through to its source. The Huddersfield Canal Society and the local authorities are working on the canals in the Colne valley. Canal societies themselves are trying to promote their local canals for long-distance walks, offering diversionary routes where the towpath is incomplete. The Stroudwater, Thames and Severn Canal Society and the Wey and Arun Canal Trust, two of the most successful, have both prepared booklets that describe the route. Elsewhere the walker is left to plot the path for himself.

The advantages of canal towpath walking quickly become clear. Apart from locks, the water does not go uphill! Where tunnels or other obstacles are encountered, the boatmen and their horses always had a way round. Sometimes a trip boat or a passing craft will offer the weary walker a lift.

There are three things which the canal walker needs to remember. The first is the Country Code – a set of useful rules which encourage people to treat the countryside with respect. Second, it is important to take a raincoat and essential to wear stout shoes. Third, it is always wise to take a map or a canal guide. Canals often wind around the countryside, and it is easy to lose one's sense of direction. The Landranger Series of Ordnance Survey maps, references for which are given at the beginning of each walk, provide further interest and lessen the danger of getting lost while exploring!

Anthony Burton, the broadcaster and writer, coined the phrase 'Backdoor to Britain' when he travelled the canals. His description is apt. They make their own paths through Britain, cutting across the landscape and sliding around the back of towns, appearing in places where one would least expect to see a waterway. The canals provide green wedges through industrial areas and link the town with the countryside. Often they are the only peaceful parts of the modern urban scene and provide a new perspective on a well-known area. Above all, they tell a story of times gone by, of feats of engineering and labour.

The walks have been chosen to cover the widest range of locations in both England and Wales. Some routes are easy – others are explorations in their own right. They can all be undertaken as a whole, or in part. Those who are short of time can bypass the difficult or lengthy sections and limit themselves to the reaches with particular visual interest. The walks cover both the old and the new – ranging from rural and agricultural via surburban to urban and industrial. Not everyone likes towns, but the urban canals have a grandure all their own and should never be disregarded simply because they are not part of the countryside. All too often you will be surprised how rural the urban sections are! Very often canals include a combination of all aspects of the environment. In much the same way rough walking, smooth walking, cycling or even sightseeing routes are all available for those who feel able to take up the challenge. For rambler or cyclist, social historian or wildlife lover, or simply for those, like most of us, who enjoy a peaceful stroll through the quiet landscape and a drink in a pleasant pub, Britain's canal heritage has something to offer everyone.

Tribulations of the artist; on Pett Level

half-mile or so, the canal and road each make a sharp double bend to provide a site for old gun emplacements. There were six such sites – three in each direction along the route to Appledore. The canal kinks inland up to Stone Bridge and Knock Farm, and then takes the opposite tack.

Stone Bridge lies at the apex of a promontory of higher land on the left, the former Isle of Oxney. To the west is the Rother valley, and to the east lie a set of drains based on High Knock channel. Once we have crossed the second lowland area we reach the village of Appledore, where a metal bridge spans the waterway. Ahead lies the National Trust section of the canal bank, a grassy walkway now taking the place of the former Military Road.

If you have time to spare, walk into Appledore village, where a single main street opens out into a broad market area, with the attractive square-towered church close by.

Further reading

F. Godwin and R. Ingrams, *Romney Marsh and the Royal Military Canal*. Wildwood House, 1980.

P.A.L. Vine, *The Royal Military Canal*. David and Charles, 1972.

The Limehouse Cut and the Lea Navigation

from Limehouse Basin (TQ 363809) via Bow Locks to
Three Mills (TQ 383828)
Map 177

The history of the Lea Navigation is a long one; the earliest records of regular navigation date back to 1220, when corn was transported from Ware to London. In 1425 the first Act of Parliament relating to the Lea became law, providing for improvements to the navigation – since then development has been continuous.

Until recent times the Lea and all its branches were tidal, almost as far as Temple Mills. The combination of regular supplies of corn, waterpower and London's ever-growing market made this whole area the site for six great tidal corn mills. One of the six, lowest but one on the river, still stands at Three Mills. In 1734 this complex included grist mills, containing six waterwheels and granaries, and a windmill on the bank. The House Mill (1776) and the Clock Mill (1817) were both tidal mills operated by the ebbing tides; the House Mill had four undershot waterwheels and the Clock Mill, with its leaning octagonal clock tower, had three. Although the mills are no longer fully operational, the buildings, together with an adjoining oast house, are still intact.

Like the Lea, Limehouse has long been associated with waterside activity. Lime burning was already in progress here in 1363 to satisfy demands for building in the City and its precincts, and there is little doubt that the name derives from this activity. Its convenient anchorage led to the growth of shipbuilding and ship repairing in Tudor times. Although this industry declined after 1700, the opening of the Limehouse Cut in 1770, linking the Lea below Three Mills and Limehouse Reach, brought in new trade, which increased when the Regent's Canal Dock was opened in 1820. The dock was designed to accommodate coastal steamers which discharged into barges and served the numerous wharfs along the Regent's Canal, as well as the Paddington Arm of the Grand Junction Canal. With the development of overseas trade Irish, Lascar, Sikh and Scandinavian seamen were seen in the

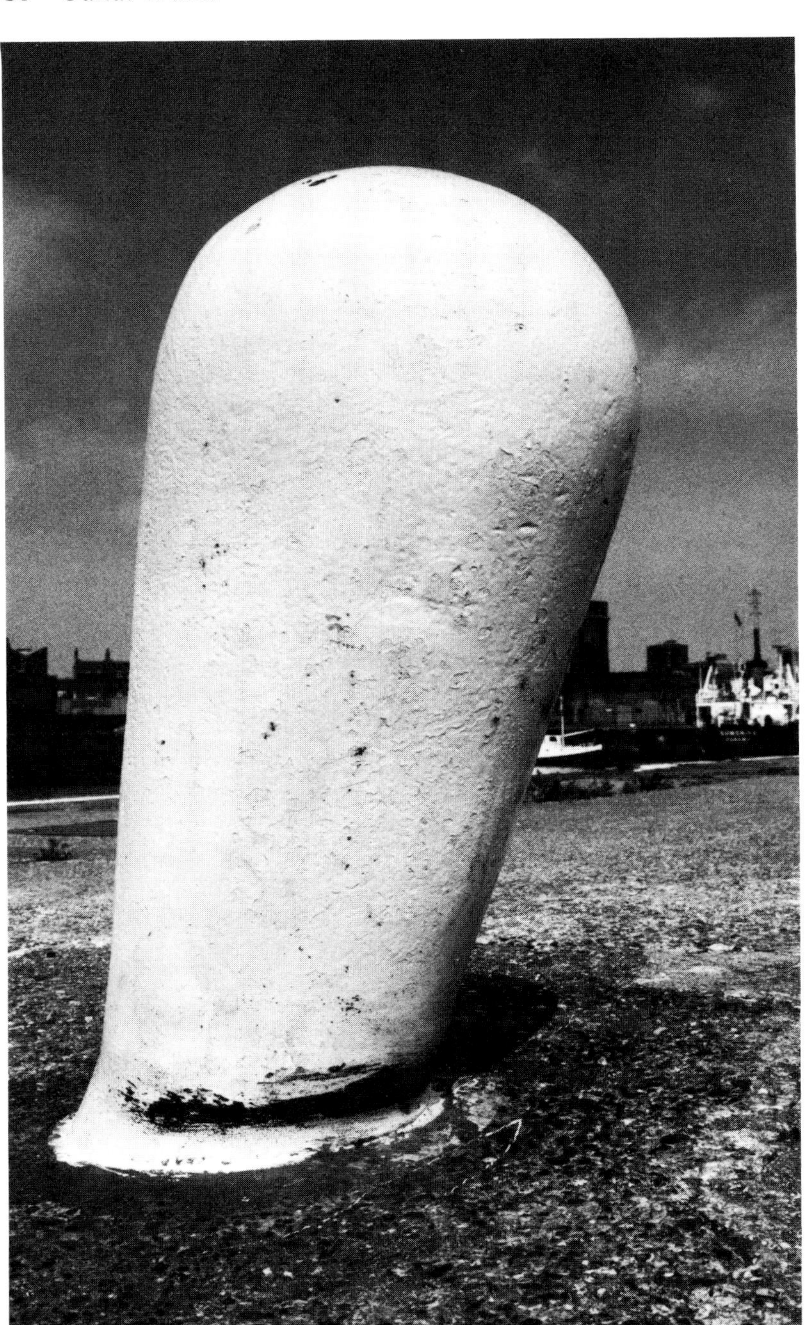

RIGHT AND OPPOSITE *In the Regent's Canal Dock*

area, and in the late nineteenth century some streets in particular became the domain of the Chinese.

Trade arriving at the upper Thames docks slowly declined, and by the early 1950s the demise of the old docks was becoming evident; the new Tilbury Docks downstream enticed shipowners away. As a result the dockland communities fell into decline, and the streets and warehouses slowly lapsed into decay. The only regular traffic now is found on the Lea Navigation, where timber lighters are brought up river from Bow Creek. Very infrequently a small coaster calls at Limehouse Dock to take away scrap metal from the only remaining active wharf.

Limehouse Dock was officially closed to general traffic in 1970. Our exploration starts there. To the north, the dock is bounded by a viaduct of the old London and Blackwall Railway. On the Thames side it is contained by a road, appropriately named Narrow Street; to the west is the approach to Rotherhithe Tunnel, and to the east the Limehouse Cut.

The dock itself has seen at least six separate stages of growth, five of them in the nineteenth century, but the last as late as 1968. In the late 1980s it is hoped to convert the whole area into a waterside village. Originally the dock was a simple basin linked in the north to the Regent's Canal by the twin Commercial Road locks, and to the Thames by a single small ship lock. A barge lock was added, parallel to the first ship lock, in 1849 when the basin was enlarged. A newer, larger, ship lock was built in 1869 to cater for the growth in size of seagoing craft; it is still in use today. The two earlier locks were later closed, and subsequently filled in. Further dock extensions came in the 1870s and a concrete jetty was built, jutting out into the basin. The last modification came in 1968 when the Limehouse Cut, until then not connected to the dock, was diverted into the basin, and its own decaying independent river lock closed and filled.

Perhaps the best place to start from is Narrow Street, where a modern swing bridge conveys traffic over the 1869 ship lock. To the west of the entrance lock lie the British Waterways Board offices. Before we enter the dock area, walk east along Narrow Street for about 50 yards to see the remains of the former entrance to the Limehouse Cut behind a cast-iron bridge parapet. A garden gate at No. 48 offers access to Thameside steps. On the northern side of the road a line of old lock cottages await demolition. On the right, an unused footpath still leads to Northey Street. The remains of the old lamps that used to light the busy lock side are now broken and swing in the breeze.

We retrace our steps westwards to the new Narrow Street swing bridge at the eastern end of which a metal gate allows access on to the lock side. The huge lock structure, 350 feet long and 60 feet wide, operates two hours before high water, if required.

The dock side today is mainly used by fishermen. Dominating the northern flank is the ornate viaduct of the former London and Blackwall Cable Railway, which it is planned to use for the route of the new docklands light railway. Before moving off towards Limehouse Cut it is worth exploring the Commercial Road locks, where the Regent's Canal joins the dock – originally they were a pair, but one has now been converted into a weir. The water here is so clear that local children use the lock as an unofficial free swimming pool. To the north of the lock, just in front of Commercial Road bridge, is a thick iron pipe used to convey water to the upper reaches of the Regent's Canal – the only way the canal could survive.

If we retrace our steps to the south-eastern corner of the dock we can see the new channel which links the Limehouse Cut to the basin itself. A metal towpath bridge crosses over the extension. The tall concrete dockside wall on the far side shows the line of the old Cut route, with the remains of a bridge still visible where the Cut once turned sharply under Northey Street.

A metal ladder, close to the eastern end of the new link canal, provides access down the 5-foot drop to the original towpath level of Limehouse Cut, on the southern side of the channel. Ahead, the line of the towpath stretches forward and soon the towpath wall is replaced by railings, which allow the residents of some new flats to enjoy the view. In front of us Britannia Bridge takes the Commercial Road over the Cut, with the ornate front of Princes Lodge visible behind mature trees, which surprisingly decorate the left bank.

Just beyond Britannia Bridge is a new tidal sluice which has been built as part of the Thames flood prevention plans. From this point onwards the towpath stretches out in a long straight line, alongside the wide Cut. Throughout the Cut the towpath is in good condition, but hardly used. Old signs stating 'Craft Trading against this Wharf' remind us of its former bustle. We pass under more road bridges and a derelict railway line with coal hoists and marshalling yards, all adding further to the air of decay.

As we near the Blackwall Tunnel approach road gulls fly overhead, their cries drowned by the traffic noise. Bow Locks can now be seen under the bridge, but the towpath ends here, on the wrong side of the main road. Ahead the path rises up a concrete slope at the top of which a 6-foot-high set of strong locked metal gates bars access to the pavement beyond. Apparently the gates are kept locked to keep vandals out. It is a pity, because it prevents the local residents from enjoying their local canal (the BWB Security Office at Bow Locks will open the gates for bona fide walkers, so long as prior notice is given; telephone 01 987 1361). A subway north of the towpath exit provides a safe route under the busy road.

Access to Bow Locks and the towpath to Three Mills is via an unsignposted access road to the south of the Cut extension. The pedestrian gates at the lock cottages are kept unlocked, even if

Bringing the bikes over. In striking contrast to the Regent's Canal dock, there is no easy official access to the Cut itself but, unsurprisingly, the locals find their own way in

the main gates are closed. Bow Locks are the focal point for the sparse remaining commercial traffic; tugs and trains of lighters can sometimes be seen here where the Lea Navigation meets the tidal Bow Creek. The mechanized double Bow Locks can only be used at around high water, as below them Bow Creek dries out at low tide. Ahead lies a smartly painted metal bridge that crosses both the Lea Navigation and the adjacent Creek and beyond it the towpath becomes the route of the main cross-London electricity supply circuit. Concrete slabs, which cover the cables, provide an even surface for the walker. We soon pass under a railway bridge. To the right is Bow Creek, which splits into two channels, while ahead a smartly grassed strand with willow trees separates the Lea Navigation from the Creek and provides a splendid foreground to the Three Mills complex behind, now in a conservation area. The old buildings stand in stark contrast to the modern brick factory wall which borders the eastern flank of the wide basin area. Looking down and across the basin at low tide, the leats for the millwheels can be seen. The Clock Mill has a cast-iron sack crane mounted on its wall, and its clock tower and the strangely shaped roof of the two oast houses form a pleasant contrast to the blocks of high-rise flats beyond.

The towpath takes us out on to an entrance road to the Three Mills complex. A public right of way passes through the forecourt area, and offers access to a towpath beside the eastern edge of Three Mills Basin, which is accessible through a narrow passage beyond the Clock Mill. Various stones on the wall here have been carved with the levels of high flood in past years. Our exploration ends here, and we return to the buses and trains by walking back along Three Mills Lane to the Tunnel Approach Road. (For those who want to explore the Mills, a more detailed visit can be arranged by contacting Hedges and Butler Ltd, telephone 01 980 7133.)

Further reading

J.G. Birch, *Limehouse Through the Ages*. Sheldon Press, 1930.

E.M. Gardner, *The Three Mills: Bromley-by-Bow*. Society for the Preservation of Ancient Buildings, 1957.

Jessie Nicholas, 'Discovering Bow Back Rivers'; a walk leaflet.

London's Industrial Archaeology, London Transport Executive publication.

The Paddington Arm, Grand Union Canal

from Paddington Basin (TQ 262818) via Little Venice, Delamere Terrace, Westbourne Park, Ladbroke Grove Kensal Green, Scrubs Lane and on to Old Oak Lane Bridge (TQ 215825)
Map 176

Very few people arriving by train at Paddington realize that the station stands next door to one of London's inland ports. Likewise few passengers who catch their bus from Praed Street know that the road got its name from William Praed, the chairman of the Grand Junction Canal Company, who built the inland port in 1801. Paddington Basin now has no public access on any side, though, and the only way to catch a glimpse of this vast unused water space is to turn north along London Street and look through a gap between the buildings on the eastern side of the station car park.

Soon after it was opened in 1801, a contemporary writer described the scene:

> A spacious basin or straight cut 400 yards long and 30 wide, has been formed with wharfs at its head and others are daily extending westwards along its sides. Behind this on the north side, is a spacious yard for a vegetable and hay and straw market with immense sheds . . . and on the south side pens are erected and provision made for a large cattle market.

Paddington Basin was the second London terminus for the Grand Junction Canal Company's route from the Midlands. The company opened their first interchange dock at Brentford in 1794, and seven years later they opened the 13-mile link from their original main line at Bull's Bridge, Southall, to Paddington to capture additional trade. The third main canal interchange basin at Limehouse Dock was not opened until 1829, when the independent Regent's Canal Company constructed their 8½-mile route from Paddington to Limehouse.

Today public access to the canal is via a hidden alley between the northern wall of the Sandell and Perkins timber yard and the concrete supports of Westway, just at the roundabout where

Bishops Bridge Road joins the Harrow Road. This little pathway quickly comes out into a magical world where narrow boats nestle beneath the arches of the many road bridges, and where fishermen sit away from the rush of London's traffic. From here the towpath passes northwards under Westway, and enters a small green courtyard with cobblestones, bollards and weeping willows.

When it was opened, the Paddington Arm came through the countryside and terminated at the outer fringe of London; since then it has attracted considerable development along its banks. However, even today the rural atmosphere is retained in the next section of the canal, Little Venice. The towpath goes northwards under another concrete bridge, and then into one of London's best-kept miniature parks – Rembrandt Gardens. In front is Little Venice, from where boats go to London Zoo and Camden Lock. A former toll cottage marks the start of the Regent's Canal.

A new way to walk a dog; by the Harrow Road

ABOVE *Like a model in concrete of Superman's flight path, Westway curves past, just over the water from Paddington General Hospital*

CENTRE TOP *Underneath Carlton Bridge*

CENTRE BOTTOM *Railway and canal in parallel, to the north of Wormwood Scrubs*

ABOVE *Underneath Westway, looking in the other direction*

To the south is the short Paddington Arm; ahead, under another ornate bridge, is the former Grand Junction Canal Company's toll house, better known to the boatmen as 'Paddington Stop'. In the centre of this waterway junction is Rat Island. This whole expanse of water is also known as Browning's Pool, after the poet, who lived nearby. The only exit from the towpath here is out through the gates of Rembrandt Gardens to Warwick Avenue. Our route follows the pavement round the northern edge of Little Venice; we start by turning left off Blomfield Road, to cross the canal at 'Paddington Stop' and, looking west, see the houseboats crowding the northern bank of the canal.

We turn right along tree-lined Delamere Terrace. After passing the concrete footbridge, we reach the open green lawns surrounding the Gothic church of St Mary Magdalene. An open footpath takes us forward across the grass to the start of the 'Canal Way'; this towpath was named as part of the 1977 Silver Jubilee celebrations, and now provides a 40-mile canalside footpath nearly all the way from Uxbridge to Limehouse. A London Tourist Board guide, *Canal Walks*, details the route and provides a useful commentary on what you will see.

The walk can be entered from either side of the Harrow Road bridge. Ahead lies the dramatic sweep of the Westway flyover. Here, and all along this section of the canal walk, the towpath is made of concrete slabs. Further ahead lies Carlton Bridge Tavern on the northern bank; beyond this bridge is Meanwhile Garden. Here a community park project created through a GLC urban environment improvement scheme provides leisure space in a former derelict area. The canal is soon crossed by a former toll footbridge, beyond which a Victorian terrace backs into the waterway, with factory walls lining the towpath edge and giving the whole canal an enclosed effect. Soon the terrace of old houses gives way to a new housing development across Harrow Road.

After a while the towpath rises over the entrance to Porta-Bella Dock. Ahead, the ornate Victorian gasholders of the Kensal Green gasworks begin to dominate the skyline, and the foliage of Kensal Green Cemetery opposite forms a marked contrast to the high brick wall on the towpath side. This reach is popular with fishermen, and the next half-mile provides a peaceful walk.

The thunder of '125' trains reminds us that the main railway line parallels the towpath in a cutting on the left for the next mile. After about half a mile, Mitre Bridge carries Scrubs Lane over the canal. Beyond it, looking south over the towpath wall, the vast expanse of Wormwood Scrubs prison can be seen. The canal actually follows a 100-foot contour for all of this length, and seats are provided at regular intervals along the towpath. After a while the canal swings northward, but soon bends to pass alongside a new factory estate. Further along, the grey girders of the angled North London Line railway bridge cross the canal. When we reach the new concrete road bridge of Old Oak Lane our walk ends; by turning off on to the road we will find buses and, some way along, Willesden Junction Station for British Rail.

Although this is a relatively short walk it epitomizes the structure of urban canals, many of which provide peaceful and almost rural walks right into the centres of towns. We are fortunate that the London borough councils have begun to recognize the recreational value of their canals.

Further reading

D. Pratt, *Discovering London's Canals*. Shire Books, 1981.
London is . . . Canal Walks. London Tourist Board, 1982.

2
South and South-west

The Thames and Severn Canal

from Sapperton Tunnel entrance (SO 934034) via Daneway, Chalford, Brimscombe Port, Bowbridge and on to Stroud (A46 road bridge) (SO 847052)
Maps 162 and 163

PRECEDING PAGE
Milepost by the A373; on the Grand Western Canal

Proposals to link the Thames and the Severn were made as early as 1610. In 1641 John Taylor is reputed to have taken a boat from the Thames up the Churn valley to near Cirencester, and thence manhandled it over the Cotswolds, to join the Frome and so gain access to the Severn. Between 1662 and 1668 various bills were proposed, but none achieved parliamentary support. The first tangible signs of success were not seen until over a century later, when the Stroudwater Navigation was opened to Stroud in 1779. It was an immediate success, and by 1781 plans were being made to link Stroud to Cricklade on the Thames. The Thames and Severn Canal Company was formed and in 1783 received an Act of Parliament to enable the construction of the canal to go ahead. Josiah Clowes was given the post of resident engineer. The canal was opened in sections, with the first being completed through to Chalford by 1785 and to Daneway Wharf in 1786. The more difficult task was the construction of Sapperton Tunnel, 3,817 yards long, which passed through some tricky ground. Even so, the first boat was able to navigate the tunnel and reach Cirencester by 1789, and the whole canal through to Inglesham Lock on the Thames, near Lechlade, was completed in November of that year.

Water supply problems and leaks dogged the canal from the outset. As a result the canal company were forced to introduce a pumping engine to keep the canal's 9-mile summit level operational. When the railways came costs began to exceed revenue, and in 1893 the company gave notice that the canal east of Chalford was to be closed. Objectors convinced the Board of Trade that such a move was illegal, and a trust was formed to reopen the waterway in 1899. However, serious leaks along the summit level still remained and the canal closed again. Gloucestershire County Council took over the waterway in 1901 and in 1904 the whole line was repaired, but by then trade had been lost. The last commercial craft cleared the summit in 1911, after which the canal slumbered and decayed. The section between Lechlade and Whitehall Bridge was officially abandoned in 1927, and in 1933 the remainder of the line to Stroud suffered the same fate. For a while the associated Stroudwater Navigation managed to struggle on, until it too was abandoned in 1954.

Our exploration examines the whole of the western section of the Thames and Severn Canal, from Sapperton Tunnel mouth to Stroud, and provides the opportunity to enjoy the edge of the Cotswolds as well.

The walk starts at Sapperton church, high up on the valley side. Our route takes us down past the church and via a side path that joins a hedged pathway leading downhill to a wooden gate. We turn left and follow the edge of a field in a westerly direction, soon reaching a spot which offers a commanding view down the deeply wooded valley of the Frome.

Some distance on, another path from the village enters the field, crossing a stile on our left. Both link to take a well-marked diagonal course down the steep valley side. We head for a clump of trees near the valley floor; by the trees a stile provides access to the tunnel portal, just to the west down another bank. The whole area above the tunnel mouth has been cleared of scrub. On the left, the old lengthsman's cottage lies overgrown and derelict. In between, we can identify the narrows where stop gates allowed the canal to be drained to plug leaks. Our path leads along beside the cottage – look back for a good view of the tunnel mouth.

The towpath is well marked and bends sharply with the canal to pick up the line of the narrow valley floor. The canal itself is reed-filled, nearly dry and overgrown. The young River Frome tunnels under the canal in a culvert and then runs parallel to the towpath under the trees to the left. As the canal slowly curves along the valley side, we can identify the concrete facing inserted to prevent leaks. At the end of our sheltered path we reach a stile and ahead, across a field, lies Daneway Inn, constructed by the canal company in 1784 to house its navvies, but converted into a pub in about 1800. The path follows the fence of the car park to Daneway Bridge, where our footpath, signposted to Chalford, leaves to the right of the bridge. Below the bridge an old wharf has been converted into a garden, while the large basin area to the left is now separated from the canal by a temporary dam. This was once one of the main wharves for the nearby sawmills.

The Sapperton Tunnel

The towpath is clear here and keeps away from the stone coping of the lock side.

The towpath now drops down to the lower level, continuing on the right bank of the overgrown canal. The path is tree-lined and provides an ideal walk on a hot summer's day. The two Lockeridge

In need of some attention; one of the locks in Lockeridge Wood

Wood Locks are soon reached, both overgrown with thick creepers concealing the deep chambers. Trees have started to grow out of the chamber walls, buckling the stones, which look likely to tumble into the canal.

Beyond these locks, the footpath continues on the right-hand edge of the now water-filled canal. Irises line the banks, taking advantage of any sun they can find. Our route continues to the two Bathurst Wood Locks. Between the upper and lower locks a track tries to cross the muddy canal bed, but soon expires in the undergrowth. At the lower lock a new wooden footbridge spans the lock chamber and carries the towpath safely to the left bank. Here again the lock is overgrown.

From the Bathurst Locks the towpath continues through the wood, and the presence of the River Frome ensures that the undergrowth is prolific along this reach. On the left of the towpath, a dry stone wall is completely overrun by a profusion of bushes and shrubs. Even the canal bed is so full of sloe bushes that it is difficult to see the other bank. Beyond the Frome, on the left, water meadows grace the central valley floor. After some way the overgrown chamber of Upper Whitehall Lock is reached. The pound below the lock is water-filled and relatively long, providing a useful reservoir after the tight flight of seven locks which extend down from the summit level. It is divided into two sections by the trim Whitehall Bridge, which carries a bridle path over the canal. The towpath goes under the left of the bridge arch, and the downstream keystone supports the inscription 'W D 1784'. It was from this bridge that the upper reaches of the canal were abandoned in 1927.

To the left, water meadows provide a protected open space for the many birds that live in the woods beyond. The stream still meanders to and fro across the valley floor, at times coming right up to the towpath edge. After a while, the canal again becomes completely overgrown, with a mass of bushes extending from bank to bank. To the right, the tall trees of Oakridge Woods line the valley side.

After some way, the towpath takes us through a wedge-shaped stile and gate and, emerging from the protective woods, continues its contour path along the right of the valley side. Crossing another stile, we soon come to Lower Whitehall Lock, below which the towpath continues along the left bank, with the river running through the fields beyond. We quickly reach the first of the two Pucks Mill locks, beside an old isolated watermill now being restored. The River Frome runs into a culvert here, at right-angles to the canal. The old lock house is in a sorry state and one can only hope that its potential for restoration will be seen before it is too late. After climbing another stile we soon reach the lock, below which an old brick bridge carries the towpath over the canal. We cross to the right bank to continue alongside a wider reach of the canal; a dry stone wall on the right protects the towpath from the rugged field beyond.

The next lock, at one stage converted into a mini-swimming pool, lies unused and begrimed. High on the valley side to the left, a railway line makes its way down towards Stroud. Ahead we can see the vast expanse of the Bakers Mill reservoir, which fills the valley floor. In its prime it held three million gallons of water and served the dual purpose of acting as a mill feeder as well as topping up the canal, which is forced to cross to the left of the valley at this point.

Just before the canal reaches Bakers Mill, it again enters a glade of mature trees. Our path continues along the right of the lock and soon dips down to pass under a solid bridge which carries the Frampton Mansell to Oakridge road over the canal. The next reach is wide, deep and clear, with a swift-flowing stream paralleling the right-hand side of the tree-lined towpath. We then reach Boulting Lock, dammed to retain the water in the concrete-lined pound above.

Along the next section of canal, a little spinney divides the towpath from the stream. The canal continues beside this stream for almost a mile before the stream drops away into a mill leat. The towpath passes an unplated milestone on the right and, on the left bank, a solid pumphouse building – the old Stroud Waterworks, which once lifted water from local wells. Beyond the pumphouse the canal bank rises sharply. Trees line this reach, which is filled with water, offering an impression of what the canal was like in its working days. On the right the river again parallels the towpath, which runs on a high causeway.

The canal bends to the right as we approach Golden Valley Lock chamber, across which a concrete dam has been built to retain the water levels. The chamber beyond is in fair condition, and is unusual in that it has two sets of quoins for lock gates at the upper end. This resulted from a practice, adopted by the company after 1841, of shortening the locks to conserve water; the shortened locks were still capable of taking 70-foot narrow boats. Our path crosses the road here to rejoin the towpath on the other side; close by are the remains of a mill race and a mill. Some of the stone cottages in the village to the right were once used by local weavers. The towpath now follows the canal past the backs of

Approaching Chalford

gardens, with the stream running in between; this length of towpath is well used by locals, as it provides a short cut through to the main road half a mile away. To the right, the stone houses of Chalford are staggered up the valley side. The canal soon passes through a more open section and we reach a set of cottages that guard Clowes or Red Lion Lock, now overgrown. Just beside the towpath is another unplated milestone, while at the tail of the lock a delightful little stone bridge spans the canal.

The small, sparkling stream continues beside the canal, but on a much lower level. On the left the canal becomes more overgrown, and in places earthslips have started to fill in the line. Our course continues along the shaded towpath through a wooded reach for about 200 yards until we emerge into the A419 trunk road at the bottom of Cowcombe Hill. Originally Bell Lock here lowered the canal so that it could pass underneath a road bridge, but road widening led to the lock being filled in and the canal being culverted.

After crossing the road, we regain the towpath on the left bank of the canal beside a factory. The canal continues for some way along the back of buildings, and in one place has been filled in, though it soon reappears. On the left the towpath is paralleled by a high stone wall, at the end of which a lane crosses the canal and obscures its route. Our path takes us up over the lane and down a steeply sloping path on the other side to pass the side of an old cottage, where a painted sign high on the wall reads: 'J.A. Miller, Coal and Stone Merchants. Boats and Barges'. Just beyond, the canal emerges again from a stone culvert with a cast-iron mile plate over its arch.

To the left is the best-preserved example of the five original 'Round House' watchman's lodges which were unique to this waterway. The building is now a private house. In its working days the ground floor was a stable, the first was a living room and the upper floor provided a bedroom. This Round House is capped with a neat conical roof. The towpath walk continues along the left bank of the canal, and in the grass we can spot a stone block with a large mooring ring. A by-road soon rises along the side of the canal and a stone wall separates the towpath from it. Just before it crosses the canal line, we reach Balingers Lock – it has been filled in and garages built over the site. The canal water passes under this obstruction by way of a culvert.

We cross the by-road and descend a flight of steps on the other side to where the towpath continues alongside the water-filled canal. The path along the next reach has been well maintained, but the canal is blocked with weeds. After a while Iles Mill Lock is reached, with a concrete dam to retain the water level above; a garden protects the right bank. Beyond the lock, a low overbridge crosses the canal and the towpath dives down underneath to enjoy a pleasant course along the next reach, with gardens bordering both sides of the canal.

Soon the railway crosses the canal and a tunnel carries our pathway through an embankment to the other side, where the canal resumes its course. Here a stone wall encloses the towpath on the left. After a short distance we reach St Mary's Lock, again in a derelict state. The towpath dives down once more and passes under the arch of a bridge.

The next section of the canal looks more like a live waterway, with the road, railway and canal all running parallel along the valley. The towpath, shaded here and there by large trees, makes an ideal walk for the next mile. After a while the river meanders across the valley floor to come close to the canal. Just beyond is Beales Lock. A bridge crosses over the canal to link to the main road close by the Victoria Inn. Below, the canal passes an industrial estate and continues along the valley floor past the end of the works, where it widens into a basin, once the site of Birds boatyard, before being culverted under the railway embankment.

Our path now makes a diversion to pass beneath an adjacent river arch, but soon rejoins the original route along the left bank of the reed-filled canal.

We now come to Bourne Lock, built wide enough to take the Severn trows through to Bird's Yard and long enough to allow Thames barges access to Brimscombe Port. Beside the lock lies the well-preserved Bourne Mill; a road passes over the tail of the lock to serve it. Our path dives down to water level to pass beneath the brick bridge, beyond which lies a small wharf area at the end of which the canal line comes to an abrupt halt: the towpath is barred by a high stone wall, the former boundary wall of Brimscombe Port, once the centre of the canal's trade. Our path takes us round the old port area by following the right bank of the River Frome. After a while the path is replaced by a works road which leads through the buildings of Hewin's Port Foundry. At the end of the site the road bears to the left, and on the right we can still spot the old stone Port Salt Warehouse near the car park. This structure is all that remains of a basin some 700 feet long and 250 feet wide, said to be capable of holding a hundred vessels at any one time. We now cross over the river bridge and turn right, continuing to a road junction where, bearing right, we reach the Ship Inn. Just beyond, our route bears left to pass alongside the Perolin Works and then takes a long, straight path.

The canal line reappears after about a quarter of a mile, and soon we reach the derelict Lewis Lock. We continue past a factory blocking the canal itself on a path beside a large caravan park. Soon the canal line re-emerges, with the railway line now running parallel, but much higher, along the hill slope to the left. We pass the Hawker Siddeley Power Plant factory on the right and reach the site of the Hope Mill Lock, beyond which lies another brick bridge, taking a lane across the canal. After this the valley floor opens out for a while and the canal passes through a grassed area to Ham Mills Lock.

The towpath passes beneath the bridge and continues on the right of the reed-filled canal. We reach a blue and white painted latticework bridge, known as Jubilee Bridge, which takes a footpath on its way to Rodborough Common, high on the hillside above. Further on we reach Griffiths Mill Lock, which has been cleared, although a lower gate is in a decayed state. Downstream from here the canal is wide, clear and deep. The towpath is a popular venue for local fishermen. Passing through a metal gate, our path soon passes under the restored red-brick arch of Stanton's Bridge. Our path continues until we reach Bowbridge Lock, beside which is a restored circular weir, and nearby an old dyeworks. This is the only reminder of the former Bowbridge Mill. The Bowbridge Lock chamber has been repaired but has no gates. Some steps now take the towpath up to the road where the canal is culverted. We cross the road to steps on the other side, where at first the towpath forms a causeway between the river and the reed-filled canal. After a while the river veers to the right to disappear behind some works which line the towpath edge. The towpath continues and, after crossing a river culvert, soon rises to an overbridge, which we cross to reach the towpath on the left bank where it doubles back under the metal span to continue its route alongside the canal.

After a while, the canal becomes a clear stretch of water and passes under an impressive brick-arched railway viaduct of 1872. Beyond the arches the canal continues along a secluded wooded cutting. Soon a timber yard lines the towpath edge and, to the right, a large ornate brick warehouse dominates the hillside overlooking the canal. The water is fairly clear here and attracts anglers. We now pass another former wharf area on the right, with a stone wharf building complete with mooring rings, to reach Wallbridge Upper Lock, the first lock on the canal. Beyond the road bridge, below the lock, the Thames and Severn Canal came to an end by connecting with the Stroudwater Navigation. Our walk ends here, beside the derelict lock. By turning right we reach the Bell Inn. Up the hill beyond lies the entrance to Stroud Station.

Further reading

M. Handford, *The Stroudwater Canal*. Alan Sutton, 1979.

M. Handford and D. Viner, *Stroudwater, Thames and Severn Canals Towpath Guide*. Alan Sutton, 1984.

H. Household, *The Thames and Severn Canal*. David and Charles, 1969.

The Kennet and Avon Canal

from Bradford-on-Avon (ST 826608) via Avoncliff, Limpley Stoke and Bathampton to Bath (ST 753643)
Maps 172 and 173

There is no doubt that the importance of Bath can be in part related to the transport link offered by the Avon to the port of Bristol. In the Middle Ages mills were built along the Avon, diverting water and hindering navigation, but by 1619 the city of Bath was actually seeking to reactivate the river to carry passengers and goods. This was finally achieved in 1727.

In 1705, Beau Nash had become Master of Ceremonies at Bath and the fame of the spa town had spread quickly. Such was the rush of people and finance that by 1729 John Wood Senior and Ralph Allen were commissioned to rebuild Bath into a city worthy of its name, and demand for local Bath stone rapidly grew.

The major local weaving industry at Bradford-on-Avon had gained its prosperity from the manufacture of high-quality cloth. The industry built up to a peak in the eighteenth century, and was constantly seeking better ways to convey its products since the local roads were not good.

The other factor which stimulated the growth of the area was Somerset coal, mainly produced from the mines around Radstock and Paulton. The need to get this coal cheaply to markets in Bath and Bristol, Bradford-on-Avon and all places east created additional pressure for the development of a local canal system.

One of the products of 'canal mania' was the building of the broad-gauge Kennet and Avon Canal. John Rennie surveyed the line and in 1794 work started at Bradford-on-Avon, but the problems of finding a contractor at first caused delay. Problems also arose when the proprietors of Sydney Gardens in Bath demanded 2,000 guineas for the right to take the canal through their property, while a series of landslips between Limpley Stoke and Bradford-on-Avon added to the costs. Water shortages also led to delays in the completion of the Widcombe flight of locks at Bath, and plans were made to link the canal to the river by a stone roadway from the wooded grounds of Sydney Gardens, as a temporary measure. In 1802 the canal became operational for the carriage of stone from Hampton Quarry Wharf to Bath, and by 1803 the line through from Bath to Foxhanger, below Devizes, was fully operational. Two years later, the Somersetshire Coal Canal was bringing its produce down to the Kennet and Avon at Dundas for transit to points beyond. The years of prosperity now began.

Bulk traffic, mainly coal, stone and agricultural products, provided the foundation for growth, but the advent of the London to Bristol railway in 1841 took away long-distance trade. Prosperity still remained through the transport of coal; it was this that enabled the canal company to sell their canal to the Great Western Railway in 1851. By the 1870s the cost of maintenance was outstripping trading returns and the closing of the Somersetshire Coal Canal in the 1890s finally deprived the Kennet and Avon Canal of this main source of revenue. The canal gradually decayed until in 1950 the through route was closed and in 1951 the Devizes locks declared unsafe. Things got steadily worse. This cycle of decline was broken by a road scheme in Bath, in the early 1970s, which prompted the replacement of a lock. Since then, section by section, the canal has been rebuilt, with the intention of getting the whole canal reopened during the next few years.

Our exploration enables us to study, at first hand, the work that has already been completed. Even if you do not wish to walk, a 'Water Bus' now operates from Bath to Claverton on certain days, but currently this does not reach Dundas or Avoncliff, which are two of the highlights that must not be missed. Consequently our walk starts from Bradford-on-Avon, to the west of which, in 1984, walking provided the most practical way of enjoying the delights of this impressive valley-side canal.

The canal at Bradford-on-Avon lies to the south of the town centre, high on the valley side, and is best approached from the Frome road. The Canal Tavern and the Barge Inn, on either side of the canal, indicate where the canal passes under the road, which crosses a humpback bridge. To the left of the canal, above the lock, is a large, low, timber and stone warehouse, now restored and used as a canal centre. To the right of it are a dry dock and landing ramp. About 100 yards above the lock, on the right-hand bank, are some old claypits, which once provided the pudding clay used to make the canal bed watertight.

The lock was restored in 1978 but remained weed-filled until

1984 when Dundas Aqueduct was restored. We approach the lower wharf area, down behind the Canal Tavern, and then follow the towpath westwards along the right bank of the canal, perched high on a man-made ledge dug out from the steep hillside which sweeps up on the left. The River Avon lies to the far right, but quickly swings across the valley floor towards the canal.

We soon pass the huge fourteenth-century tithe barn. This tremendous stone building with slated roof, which has been restored by the Department of the Environment, lies at the southern edge of the Barton Farm Country Park that now encompasses the wooded valley floor south of the River Avon and parallels the canal at the foot of the steep valley side. To the right, a grass-covered stone wall separates the canal from the country park. After a while it is possible to see across the valley floor and trace the course of the Avon as it flows through the wooded fields below. Beyond the river, the railway follows the northern edge of the valley floor.

The canal bank along this reach is unstable, and occasionally large trees are dislodged. Further along, drainage sloughs emerged from underneath the canal embankment, sending little streams to link with the Avon below. The canal hugs the contour and the towpath is quite muddy. In places a diversion must be made. The valley gradually narrows, with steep banks on either side. After a while the canal swings to the left. Stop plank grooves by the bridge offer protection in emergencies. Beyond them the canal follows its valley-side path.

The towpath now leads us along a stone wall and beside Becky Addy Wood on the valley side. The walk here is very peaceful though muddy. Soon we can glimpse the impressive stone Avoncliff Aqueduct as it carries the canal across the valley. The main arch of the aqueduct has a sag, which occurred at the time it was built; later repairs, in a patchwork of different-coloured bricks, tend to detract from this otherwise attractive structure. Just before the aqueduct the Avon passes over a wide mill weir, and the noise of the flowing water echoes around the valley.

We emerge from our wooded walk to reach the hamlet of Avoncliff and ahead the canal makes a sharp bend, to the right, to cross the aqueduct. The canal sides here are stone-walled and recently rebuilt, and the aqueduct itself has been relined with concrete to stop leaks.

Restoration of the Avoncliff Aqueduct, 1980. A concrete trough is being inserted inside the shell of the original stonework

We can walk across the aqueduct to study the weir and the mills below. The two Flock Mills, one on either side of the river, were water-powered. The one on the northern edge lies derelict; the more solid mill to the right has been converted into a private house. To the far left is Avoncliff railway halt.

We now cross to the left bank of the canal, gaining access to the towpath by walking down the sloping road to the Cross Guns public house and then doubling back along a footpath which leads under the southernmost arch of the aqueduct. We rejoin the left-hand towpath to cross over the aqueduct. Once across the valley, the canal turns sharply to the left to resume its course along a ledge carved out from the wooded valley side. The railway runs parallel to the canal along the next reach, some 20 feet below the canal bed. The new cross-section profile of the canal is best seen at the Avoncliff turn, where stop planks can be inserted just beyond an old wharf area.

The canal follows a straight course for about a quarter of a mile; the far valley side is wooded until the canal reaches open fields on the right, curving sharply to follow the valley side. After the bend, it passes under Winsley Bridge. Ahead, the valley side is tree-covered.

The canal now follows the wooded valley side again. Far in the distance the village of Limpley Stoke can just be seen where the valley turns to the north. As we get closer, the flat storage area of Muirhill Quarry Wharf is clearly defined, with the line of the old tramway, now converted to a track, running diagonally down the steep valley side from the derelict stone quarry above. Beyond a cottage on the far bank some stop gates were provided to shut off the canal in case of a breach. The pathway along this reach is wide and clear, although muddy in places; shaded by tall trees on either side, it makes a pleasant sheltered walk.

After about a mile, the canal curves to the right. The valley is quite narrow here. In the valley floor a sawmill building straddles the side of the river by a weir some 30 feet below. The railway now runs parallel to the river, and beyond lies the village of Limpley Stoke. An old bridge carries a road over the river here. Soon steep fields replace the trees on the right-hand bank. Ahead, the ornate stone bridge at Limpley Stoke crosses the canal line; beside it, on the towpath side, an old stone cottage stands next to a modern white house. Stop planks can be inserted under the bridge, which marks the end of the concreted section. The next reach used to be reed-filled and quite overgrown.

The canal continues north along the valley side. The towpath is narrower here, but less muddy. A hedge separates the towpath from a farm track, and on the right a row of trees stands between the canal side and some fields, which soon give way to the extensive Conkwell Woods. Our path soon becomes muddy again, but then enters a wooded reach which obscures the view across the valley beyond. Recently the canal has been dredged, but water lilies cover the surface in places. After a while we can see across the valley again and note where the embankment of a former railway used to climb up a side valley. Now a busy road crosses over the entrance to this valley on a high viaduct.

Stop gates narrow the canal ahead and, beyond, a strange shed-like structure seems to be built across the canal. As we get closer, it can be seen that the canal turns sharply left in front of it and the structure is on the site of a former wharf. Ahead is the Dundas aqueduct, with its ornate balustrades and a towpath on either side. Originally the far towpath carried a tramway from Conkwell Quarry high above the canal on the right-hand valley side. A flight of private steps allows access to the river bank below and provides a good view of the vast three-arched structure.

On the far side of the aqueduct is Dundas Wharf, where a crane stands beside a small warehouse. The wharf once formed the junction with the Somerset Coal Canal, which continued along the eastern valley side. Over the garden wall to the left we can see the former lock cottage, which controlled entry to the canal. In the middle of the cottage garden the unmistakable stone sides of a narrow lock now border a long, narrow rose garden, set in the centre of the flat lawn: this was the stop lock of the Coal Canal.

Our route skirts round the left of Dundas Wharf and heads northwards to a bridge. Here we cross to join the towpath on the right bank. The wooded Avon valley continues northwards for nearly a mile, steeply banked on either side. The canal here is deep, wide and clear, and boats regularly ply along it to Dundas Wharf.

Further along the hedge disappears and we get a wonderful view down the valley. After this the canal curves behind a knoll and soon the white-painted Millbrook swing bridge spans it. High on the valley side, beyond the fields, the traffic zooms along the Warminster road. The canal soon passes a small valley, down which a small stream feeds into the waterway.

As the towpath passes under Claverton Bridge, the rope burns in the stonework edges are clearly visible. Just beyond, a path leads down the steep valley side and passes over the railway to provide access to Claverton Water Pump, a unique feature of the canal and well worth a visit. It is open for viewing on most weekends. The waterwheel-powered pump, built in 1813, lifts water from the River Avon below to the canal, some 47 feet above. Since the structure is now an industrial archaeological site, electric pumps have been provided to take over the regular task of feeding the canal. The old water pump is only operational on certain weekends during the summer months.

Continuing along the towpath, we pass over the leat that supplies the water from the pump to the canal. Over the towpath fence, one can see through the door of the pumphouse below and watch the beam engines moving up and down. From this point the canal takes up a more even profile along the hillside and passes through sloping meadows. We soon pass a winding hole. On the far side of the valley, the palatial Warleigh Manor stands on the wooded valley edge.

Soon the railway and river swing out to the centre of the valley floor, while the canal veers round to follow the curve of the valley side. As we round a bend we see Harding's Bridge, which offers an access link to the fields beyond. For the next mile the canal passes through thinly wooded fields, with thicker woods higher up the valley side on the left. Beyond, the main road rises slowly to seek a path round the hilltop.

We then reach another narrow section of the valley where the canal, railway and river, in descending order, feel their separate ways through the available space. Further along the valley we can see the village of Bathford. A pile of stop planks lies beside the canal, ready for any emergency. Ahead is Hampton Quarry Wharf, where a swing bridge crosses the canal. Up the hillside to the left we can just make out the diagonal line of the former tramway, which once carried stone down from the quarry to the wharf. The wharf area is now a well-used mooring.

Beyond the bridge is a water point for canal craft. After some distance, the canal swings to the left round a spur, offering a fine view over the valley to Bathford. The canal then follows the contour and swings right to pass around King Edward's School playing fields on the left. The towpath is well used along this section.

The canal now heads westwards to the village of Bathampton with its tree-lined village wharf, beyond which a stone bridge carries a local road over the canal. We soon pass Bathampton church, which lies to the right of the canal, with a delightful green picnic area beside the towpath in the grounds of the George Inn. On the left bank Chapel Row lies beside the canal, with stone cottages on either edge. On the left we soon pass the former Harbutt's Plasticine factory and beyond it, along the left bank, some modern detached houses. After another narrow section, houses give way to meadows as the canal feels its way towards Bath, passing under Candy's Bridge. Ahead lies Bath; the railway line and the river below also head for the town along the same valley.

After passing another swing bridge we reach a long, straight stretch of towpath. Soon the terraces of Bath begin to dominate the valley. Walling now protects the canal towpath from the railway below as they draw closer together. Both now curve to the left, and we reach Darlington Wharf.

Beyond the far end of the wharf area, tucked into the side of the hill, is the ornate entrance to Sydney Gardens Tunnel No. 2. The main A36 road passes diagonally overhead. The towpath goes through the tunnel on the right-hand side. Beyond the tunnel, two white-painted cast-iron bridges span the canal. The first is a skew arch with diamond-shaped trelliswork on the edges. Beyond is the other – more linear, yet similarly ornate – bridge, dated 1800. These link the two halves of the wooded Sydney Gardens.

Ahead, the grand style of the former Canal Company headquarters, Cleveland House, stands over the second tunnel mouth. The towpath passes under Cleveland House, through the tunnel along the canal side. There is a trapdoor in the roof of the tunnel, through which packets could be lowered from the company offices to passing craft.

Just south of the tunnel the towpath changes sides and follows the wooded left-hand bank. Ahead is the site of Sidney Wharf, where old warehouses still stand. Just beyond, the balustraded Sydney Wharf Bridge crosses the canal.

We cross Sydney Wharf Bridge and then descend some steps to rejoin the towpath. The path from here on is tarmaced and

Sydney Gardens Tunnel No. 2, leading to . . .

provides a wonderful entry into the town. Tiers of solid, stone-built houses dominate the valley side. After a while the Hugh Baird and Sons stone-built malthouse is seen lying alongside a former wharf on the left bank. A little further along, an old stable building stands alongside the canal. Ahead are the large double gates of the Bath Top Lock. Beside the lock, and on the towpath edge, is an old lock keeper's cottage which still carries the sign of the Bath Humane Society.

At the tail of the lock a white-painted iron footbridge crosses the canal. Beyond, on the right, is the Kennet and Avon Canal information office in an old canalside building.

Our path continues down along the towpath to the second lock, before which a long side pond extends along the backs of the houses on the left. Below this second lock, the canal widens into a pool. To the right stands an ornate stone chimney, all that remains of a former pumphouse; the site is now used as a yard for the Canal Trust. We soon pass another deep, wide lock and go

. . . the cutting through Sydney Gardens, expensively redesigned with much use of rusticated stonework and ornamental cast iron, to look like an extension of the pleasure gardens themselves. The adjacent and later railway cutting has nothing like the same degree of style

over a road, where another slope takes us down beside the sweep of the canal as it curves to Wash House Lock.

Soon steep, sloping alleys lead down to the street below. We pass another lock and an ornate bridge to where the canal curves at right-angles to pass into the new Bath Deep Lock, which, with a drop of nearly 20 feet, must be one of the deepest canal locks in England. It was built in 1976 to replace the original lock and a second lock, that formerly stood below, and which were obliterated in a road development scheme. Our path takes us along the side of the deep lock and out to the new road bridge which spans its tail.

The towpath now passes along the left edge of the canal, down under the new span to the basin and Widcombe Lock beyond. Beside this lock are the remains of Thimble Mill and its tall chimney, originally built to house the coal-powered steam pumping station to raise water from the Avon to a basin beside the second pumping station higher up the flight. Now this building awaits another use. In the interim its wall supports a plaque reading: 'British Waterways Board Widcombe Locks, restored at the expense of the City of Bath and the Kennet and Avon Canal Trust 1969–1976'. A tiny stone-arch bridge takes a lane over the tail of the lock, beyond which is the River Avon. To the right the towpath leads up to North Parade Road bridge, beyond which are the Pulteney Bridge and weir. Our route takes us to the left along the bank of the river where a girder bridge (called Halfpenny Bridge because it was formerly a toll bridge) brings us to Bath Station.

Our walk has covered the prettiest part of the Avon valley – what is so remarkable is that the whole 9½ miles of canal between Bradford-on-Avon and Bath Top Lock is on a single level: quite a feat for such hilly country. It is only in the last half mile that the canal is lowered 65 feet through the Widcombe Locks.

Further reading

K.R. Clew, *The Kennet and Avon Canal*. David and Charles, 1973.

K.R. Clew, *Wessex Waterway*. Moonraker Press, 1978.

'Bath to Bathampton' – Towpath Guide No. 2, Kennet and Avon Canal Trust.

The Grand Western Canal

from Tiverton Wharf (SS 963124) via Sampford Peverell and Burlescombe to Loudwells (ST 074196)
Map 181

One of the most talked about schemes of the canal era was that of a link between the Bristol and the English Channels. In 1796 an Act of Parliament was obtained to construct such a canal, with three branches – to Cullompton, Tiverton and Wellington – but owing to the Napoleonic Wars the venture was dropped. In 1810 the route was resurveyed by John Rennie and the proprietors decided to build the canal in sections. Work started on the summit level, and in 1814 the Loudwells to Tiverton section was opened to take advantage of the local trade from the quarries at Westleigh. The only other section to be built was the link from Loudwells to Taunton; this was opened in 1838, but never became successful. Problems with its vertical lifts affected its profitability, and it was closed in 1869.

The Grand Western Canal still reaches Tiverton, with its terminus high on the valley side overlooking the town. It is approached from the town centre by going up Canal Hill. The wharf area itself is now a picnic site, and the old lime kilns are carefully preserved to show people how the lime and coal were conveyed from the boats to the top of the kilns, and the burnt lime extracted from underneath ready for transport elsewhere. Throughout its working life the canal was used extensively for conveying stone from the quarries near Burlescombe to wharfs along the route, where it was processed. In 1848 the railway reached Tiverton and the canal, which was becoming increasingly expensive to maintain, declined in competitiveness and was virtually abandoned by 1924 after a major leak occurred.

In 1971, following many years of public concern about the state of the canal, it was acquired by Devon County Council from the British Waterways Board for use as a country park. Since then it has been restored to its former glory, involving the clearance of vast quantities of mud and silt, the reflooding of the mile-and-a-half dry section near Halberton, and extensive repairs to an aqueduct on the line. Now the Tiverton Canal Basin area provides an ideal picnic site and the horse-drawn boats that

Leaving Tiverton. One towpath user . . .

convey day trippers along the first reach ensure that many enjoy the newly restored waterway.

A flight of steps links the lower picnic area to the canal side, from where the full extent of the basin can be seen. Across the water are the stables of the horses that draw the trip boats which go regularly along the canal. Rowing boats can be hired in the basin area.

We set off, turning west along the canal to start our walk on the well-maintained towpath. The canal is of typical contour construction as it leaves the town, cut from the bank of the valley, with the towpath carefully placed on the downhill side to create a protective barrier for the canal itself. The towpath is used both as the route for the horses that pull the trip boats and as a cycle track. After a short distance the modern wooden William Authors Bridge spans the canal, linking the estates on either bank. Regular access points are provided to the various small residential culs-de-sac lying below the level of the canal.

We soon reach Tidcombe Bridge, where the masons' marks are clearly identified on the blocks of stone. Beyond this bridge the waterway has a much more rural atmosphere.

The canal now winds its way through the heart of the countryside, protected on either side by mature trees. After a while the fine stone of Manley Bridge is reached, followed by a stretch where open fields line the right-hand bank, but on the towpath side a hedge protects the canal. We round another bend and ahead is a bridge taking a lane over the canal at East Manley. Just beyond, a winding hole provides a turning point for the trip boats. From here the towpath is less well used, although still carefully mown. The canal soon crosses an aqueduct and then follows a contour around the valley edge. Water lilies almost cover the whole surface of the canal along this reach.

We soon reach the stone-arched Crownhill, or Change Path, Bridge; beyond it is a small wharf area. At this bridge the towpath switches to the right bank. Soon we can see the village of

. . . and another, an Irish draught horse resting before the return journey into Tiverton, with a valuable cargo of holidaymakers. For this labourer's benefit, the towpath is kept neatly mown along the grassy stretch to the west of Halberton

Halberton in the valley below. Passing under the A373 Tiverton to Wellington road, the canal turns sharply to the left alongside a larger wharf area. From this point the canal follows a contour line in a complete U-shaped circuit around a small valley before working its way back towards Halberton. In one place, the loop passes through a short tree-lined cutting. After completing the loop, the canal passes under the brick Sellake Bridge and behind the village. Along this reach, wild yellow water lilies decorate the surface of the canal.

After Greenway Bridge, the canal passes into a short wooded cutting at the end of which is Swing Bridge, now a fixed metal span. Just beyond, the canal crosses a minor valley on a dramatic embankment, some 50 feet high and 300 yards long. From the embankment, looking to the right, we get a dramatic view over the low-lying vale. The canal now enters a short cutting leading to Rock Bridge, another wharf area with an adjacent stone quarry, and then takes a high contour line, with very good views over the vale to the right. At the end of the next reach is Battens Bridge, with the outline of the village of Sampford Peverell visible along the skyline. The canal in fact cuts through the centre of the village, and old Canal Company records show that some of the village had to be demolished when it was originally built.

After the wharf the canal is led under a brick-arch bridge and proceeds along the backs of some houses, across another embankment, to leave the village. Once beyond Buckland Bridge, the canal briefly re-enters the countryside, but the rural charm is quickly broken by a stark new concrete bypass bridge that crosses the canal. However, once Holbrook Bridge is reached the rural peace returns, and the canal continues to wind along on its contour path. We soon reach Ayshford Bridge and to the left, beyond it, is a delightful little chapel behind which lies an impressive stone manor house.

The towpath enters a shallow tree-lined cutting, and a long straight reach leads through the Westcott Bridge, beyond which in the distance are the stone quarries from which much of the cargo carried on the canal was derived. A by-road crosses the canal at Ebear Bridge, beyond which the canal begins to bear to the right, initially heading towards Burlescombe, but suddenly changing direction to curve left towards Canonsleigh quarries. The ninth milestone is passed just before the canal embankment crosses a little stream by an impressive stone aqueduct. Then, just before it reaches the main Bristol to Exeter railway line, the canal bears sharply to the left. At this point, on the left bank, a complicated weir takes off the excess water.

We soon reach a rusty metal bridge which once carried the Westleigh tramway across the canal, linking the quarry with the railway line. A little further on is Fossend Bridge with before it, on the left bank, another derelict canal wharf, and beyond, the ivy-covered remains of an Augustinian nunnery. After this point the canal starts to enter a wooded cutting, following a straight course under Fenacre Bridge, before which a spring provides one of the sources of water for the canal. The canal now continues on to Whipcott Bridge, an impressive stone structure. From this point the canal narrows and soon the entrance to Waytown Tunnel is reached, almost camouflaged beneath the undergrowth. Here the towpath rises to cross over the road above and just as quickly goes down the other side. At first the towpath runs at a high level, but it soon drops down to reach the canal side.

The canal now continues in its wooded cutting for some distance, and then ends abruptly in a small stone basin, now the home of swans and ducks. This was the first of the locks on the line to Taunton. From this point a lane returns to the main road, and exploration ends here.

Throughout its length the canal is on a single level; it provides what must be one of the best examples of the linear country park in England. It is now maintained and operated by the Devon County Council, who must be commended for the efficient way in which they keep it in such good condition for everyone to enjoy.

Further reading

H. Harris, *The Grand Western Canal*. David and Charles, 1973.

'Grand Western Canal', booklet published by Devon County Council.

3

East Midlands

The Market Harborough Arm

from Market Harborough (SP 727879) via Foxton to Foxton Locks and Inclined Plane (SP 702898)
Map 141

PRECEDING PAGE *The Market Harborough Arm, approaching the Foxton Flight*

The present canal route between Foxton and Market Harborough is the result of a compromise. In 1792 the Leicester and Northamptonshire Union Canal Company planned a tunnel through the Bowden Ridge at Foxton to provide access to the Welland valley – with their main line subsequently meandering off towards Northampton and an Arm, passing Lubenham, terminating at a planned basin in Market Harborough. However, just two years later the company was already short of funds and realized the need to omit the potentially expensive Foxton Tunnel. In 1794 they unveiled revised plans, with their canal running to the north of Bowden Ridge along the contour line from Foxton to Bowden Hall, whence the revised route circled through Great Bowden, in an easterly arc, to pass through Market Harborough and on to Gartree, from which point the canal followed the contour path around the Welland valley, circling Lubenham, and onwards to Northampton. This plan was strongly contested by a local landowner, Sir John Palmer, who accused the canal company of breaking their word by even considering a deviation through Foxton village. The dispute quickly became academic because the canal company had to terminate its works in 1797 at Debdale Wharf, just over a mile north of Foxton, because of shortage of funds.

When in 1804, interest was revived in continuing the canal and linking it up with the Grand Junction Canal the company's engineer, John Barnes, recommended that instead of going on to Market Harborough the canal should rise up a flight of locks at Foxton and then continue south-west to join the Grand Junction Canal near Long Buckby. Initially this plan was not accepted and Thomas Telford was employed to survey a new line. He proposed a lower but longer route, via the south side of the Northamptonshire uplands, to link the Grand Junction at Norton. This envisaged following the earlier deviation route through Foxton to Bowden Hall, then a cutting through the ridge to Gartree and then continuing onwards across the Welland valley. This scheme was approved in 1804, and the cutting through the ridge beyond Bowden Hall was quickly started. Funds again run short and, to cut their losses, the Leicester and Northamptonshire Union Canal Company simply decided to follow the contour line into Market Harborough and build a basin. As a result the intended main line, the 'Old Union', became the 'Harborough Arm', which opened on 13 October 1809.

Barnes's earlier idea of a through route via Foxton and Norton Junction was subsequently developed by the Grand Junction Canal Company engineer, Benjamin Bevan, and work began on it in 1810. It included the construction of the spectacular Foxton flight of ten locks, in two staircases of five, separated by a passing pound, which were completed by 1 October 1812. The remainder of the route was not opened to through traffic until 9 August 1814. This new link, the 'Grand Union', was never a financial success and in 1893–94, together with the 'Old Union', it was purchased by the Grand Junction Canal Company who had plans to improve the canals and capture more trade.

In July 1896 they decided to build an inclined plane at Foxton to overcome the serious congestion that occurred on the ten-lock flight. It was designed by Gordon Cale Thomas and patented in 1897, and the completed lift was opened on 10 July 1900. Unfortunately, a variety of problems dogged the lift throughout its short working life and it was last operated in March 1911. The whole unique structure was finally sold for scrap and dismantled in 1928.

In 1929 the Grand Junction, the Regent's and the Birmingham and Warwick Canal Companies amalgamated to become the 'new' Grand Union. This company subsequently purchased the Leicester Canal and the Loughborough and Erewash Navigations, to complete the ownership of the whole through route from the Thames to the Trent and beyond.

Our exploration starts at Market Harborough, on the 'Old Union' line. Like Tiverton, this is one of those towns where the canal is not down in the river valley, where you could expect it to be, but halfway up a hill, on the outskirts of the central area.

The basin at Market Harborough is approached along a short 'private road' called Union Row. The basin is now the home of Harborough Marine Ltd, builders of pleasure craft. Their boats and visiting hire craft make the basin even busier today than it was in its commercial heyday. The basin itself is now arrayed

At Market Harborough Basin, where business is booming

with finger-like jetties and on a Saturday morning, when the hire fleet is in, there is little space to spare. Slipways provide access to the water and also to the boatbuilders' sheds.

Access to the towpath is gained by following a muddy track to the rear of the Harborough Marine Works. Across the canal here, older houses line the banks. The neatly trimmed grassy towpath follows the left bank of the canal, which is quite steeply banked along this reach. On the non-towpath side the slope continues upwards to the crest of the hill.

Every few hundred yards the canal narrows, and stop-plank grooves are visible; in other cases the narrows are the sites of access bridges that have long since gone. After a while a new pathway links the towpath to a housing estate below, and a spill weir makes an exit under the towpath edge.

From here the towpath becomes more open and, looking to the left, we can appreciate how high the canal is above the surrounding area. In these circumstances it is easy to understand the problems the early canal builders faced, and it is no wonder that Telford planned a 70-foot-high aqueduct across the Welland valley floor!

The outskirts of Market Harborough are soon reached by the canal as it gently snakes its way along the contour line. Just before we reach the first bridge there is a layby on the right bank of the canal, offering a neat mooring for the members of the Old Union Canal Society. It is an ideal spot, with a magnificent view. At this point there is also a Grand Junction Canal Company milepost – Leicester 24 miles – together with a Grand Union Company boundary marker post.

Just beyond the footbridge, on the towpath side, is a spot where dredgings have been dumped on to an adjacent field – the canal company exercising its right to deposit spoil on adjacent land. The canal is wide and deep along this reach, but the peace is broken by the constant hum of traffic on the A6, only a field away. Across the fields to the west, Gartree prison seems large and daunting. We soon reach the first road bridge over the canal, which lies just behind the workshop of Smith's Garage and acts as a roving bridge, as the towpath changes to the right-hand bank beyond this point.

Standing on the bridge, and looking back towards Market Harborough, it is interesting to see how the canal engineers had to make a low embankment to retain the contour line. It was at this spot, when the canal was being built, that the decision was taken to terminate the line at Market Harborough, rather than proceed to Northampton.

The canal now edges into a shallow cutting and soon turns sharply under the new A6 bridge, after which it enters the deep cutting which was the main feature of Telford's plan. The cutting, which is remarkably wide, gradually gets deeper, to a maximum of some 40 feet. Halfway along, a 4-mile marker (from Foxton Junction) is set in the bank at the side of the towpath. From this point the cutting begins to sweep in a wide arc until at the end one can see Saunt's Bridge, named after a local landowner. Beyond this bridge the canal resumes a contour course, this time along the left of the Welland valley.

Ahead, through the trees, the outline of Great Bowden Hall emerges and beyond Bowden Hall Bridge a rather large black pipe crosses the canal and mars the view. Soon, however, we reach a point where the Welland valley stretches out below and to the east, offering an exceptionally good view.

The canal gradually begins to turn west and take a course towards Foxton. A 3-mile post is soon passed, almost hidden from view in a towpath hedge, and beyond lies a three-quarter-mile reach, lined with oak trees which provide a very effective back-drop to the canal. The canal here is carved out of the fairly steep hillside, and the land below the towpath quickly falls away to the valley floor.

Passing under the rebuilt Gallows Hill Bridge, the canal swings south but then bends again to follow the contour line. A cleft in the hill ahead forces the canal to turn sharply, and it widens here before continuing its course towards Foxton. A brick-arch bridge spans the line, and beyond it a spill weir takes surplus water into a hidden channel under the towpath and down through a nearby brook to the river below. At the brow of the hill, the floodlight poles of Gartree prison seem very close. Further along, another arched accommodation bridge crosses the canal with, beyond, the 1-mile post. From here the tower of Foxton church stands above the trees on the hillside above the village that lies below the canal line.

The canal now swings round to the right to the Foxton swing bridge, with its distinctive No. 4 plate. Another brick bridge soon spans the canal. Passing under the bridge we make our way towards Foxton Locks, which at first are hidden by the trees that now cover much of the site of the old incline plane. Just before we reach the array of buildings on the left bank, which surround the old wharf at the bottom of the locks, a bridge carries a private road over a canal arm. The keystone of the bridge bears the date 1899. This was the entrance to the lower level of the inclined plane – it now provides a safe mooring for some residential boats. A few yards further on we gain a spectacular view up the ten-lock flight. At the bottom, a neat brick bridge carries another towpath over the entrance channel. To reach it we have to follow our towpath a few more yards to where a roving bridge takes us over the canal. Just before this bridge, a stream passes right under the canal in a culvert. From the roving bridge, one can study the buildings on the bottom lock wharfside. Originally these included a carpenter's shop, a blacksmith's forge and the offices of the canal company, as well as the old lock house. Now the site is a boat yard.

The lock flight at Foxton always seems to be a hive of activity – with boats coming down and others waiting to go up. There is so much to see that visitors regularly line the bridge over the bottom of the locks on summer weekends, while others examine the locks or tour the remains of the Incline Plane.

At the junction by the bottom lock, a signpost guides the boaters for their onward course. We pass over the bridge at the bottom of the locks, and note in the front garden of the lock house, on either side of a blue front door, a 'Leicester 18 miles' marker post and a G J C boundary post. Just beyond the lock house is the Bridge 61 public house. An array of old cast-iron canal signs lines the outside wall, while in the bar a splendid collection of old prints shows the Inclined Plane when it was operational. The Foxton Incline Plane Trust, who are currently raising funds to develop their restoration work, have a small exhibition of trucks and rails adjacent to the pub, on the side of the pathway leading to the Plane site.

From the pub we can either explore the remains of the Incline Plane, or slowly stroll up the side of the lock flight, examining the reeded side ponds as we go. From the top of the flight a lock cottage and adjacent footpath offer a remarkable view back down the locks to the valley beyond.

From the footbridge at the top of the locks a footpath leads across to the old boilerhouse, which once powered the Incline Plane. This is presently being rebuilt to act as a museum and

At Foxton wharf

information centre. By returning to the top of the locks and following the towpath to the right of the canal, it is easy to gain access to a lane for the return walk to Market Harborough.

Further reading

A. Faulkner, *The Grand Junction Canal*. David and Charles, 1973.

M. Matts, editor and publisher, *The Foxton Story*; also *The Canal at Foxton*.

P. Stevens, *The Leicester Line*. David and Charles, 1972.

'The Foxton Leaflet', Leicestershire County Council.

Foxton Locks and Barge Lift, Council for the Preservation of Rural England.

The Lift Trail, Foxton Inclined Plane Trust.

The Old Union Canals of Leicestershire and Northamptonshire, Old Union Canal Society.

4

Central and West Midlands

The Stratford-upon-Avon Canal

from Bancroft Basin, Stratford-upon-Avon (SP 205548) via Wilmcote, Preston Bagot and Lowsonford, to Kingswood Junction, Lapworth (SP 187708)
Maps 139 and 151

PRECEDING PAGE *The canal idyll, to the north of Wootton Wawen on the Stratford-upon-Avon Canal*

The Stratford-upon-Avon Canal and the Wey Navigation are the only two navigable inland waterways run by the National Trust. However, even as this is written the Trust is seeking to divest itself of responsibility for the Stratford Canal. Why this should be will be evident once the exploration is completed – yet many people will argue that the Trust should continue to retain and maintain this part of the national heritage, whatever the immediate practical costs.

The Stratford Canal was one of those waterways which from the outset was dogged by financial problems. It was planned to link Birmingham to the Avon Navigation at Stratford. Although Acts were granted in 1793 to allow the canal to be built, it was not until 1812 that construction on the southern section started at Kingswood. The canal was through to Wootton Wawen in 1813 and opened to Stratford in June 1816. By then a rival canal link to the Severn valley was operational and potential traffic was being lost. Railways took more traffic from the 1850s, and the Great Western bought out the canal company at that time. Thereafter the decline set in. The last commercial craft reached Stratford in 1933, and from then the central wharf area gradually reverted to a lilypond and the canal fell into decay.

In 1958, Warwickshire County Council sought to apply for abandonment of the canal to facilitate the replacement of a decayed bridge at Wilmcote. What followed is now part of the annals of waterways history, the details of which are recorded elsewhere. By the combined efforts of local and national bodies and individuals the whole length of the canal was renovated and then reopened on 11 July 1964.

Our exploration starts in the centre of Stratford-upon-Avon at Bancroft basin, close by the old tramway bridge.

At first there seems no outlet to the canal but by crossing Clapton Bridge Road one can see how the canal slides behind the backs of buildings, both old and new, on its secret path out of town. To get to the towpath one has to follow the Warwick Road past the bus garage to beyond the Red Lion Inn, on the right, where there is a bridge over the canal. On the far side, an opening takes a path to Bridge Cottage, from which access can be gained to the towpath as it creeps under the Warwick Road bridge. Immediately above the bridge is the bottom of a flight of four locks which lower the canal to the basin level.

The first section of the towpath, alongside the locks, is well used, although the surrounding areas are overgrown and down at heel, and it takes the walker past those parts of the town the tourist never sees. The canal for the most part seems ostracized – even the nettles by the path side have an unwelcoming sting. At the next bridge the towpath ducks under Great William Street, beyond which is a lock. One has to be very wary here for the towpath under the bridge can become an overspill for the lock if someone has left a gate paddle open further up the line! Above the lock, the towpath is partly overgrown and a little damp, making one's going difficult under two bridges which span the canal. At bridge No. 65 a gate leads out to the Birmingham road. Above the lock beyond and on the right is the first boatyard of the canal. The towpath still continues along the right-hand bank and for a while offers an acceptable path past the old Stratford gasworks site, soon reaching a pair of old railway bridges, the second of which carries the Stratford to Hatton branch line. Once beyond these bridges we reach the new industrial area of Stratford – where spacious new works have spread out over former poor-quality farming land. None is close to the canal, which is now protected by overgrown hedges. The canal soon passes under a new bridge which carries the industrial estate road and from this point the towpath becomes very tricky. In places the bank has crumbled away; elsewhere trees try to force the unwary walker into the canal. One has to feel one's path gingerly through the undergrowth in fear of slipping into the canal. Ahead, the isolated Bishopton Lock is soon seen, where the chamber has been completely rebuilt in concrete. Here on the left bank dog roses cover the bushes. This marks the edge of Stratford; for the rest of its route the canal enjoys the Warwickshire countryside.

Above the lock the canal veers to the left, soon reaching Bishopton Lane road bridge where the towpath is replaced by an access road and provides the best walking surface, so far, along the canal. This length is extensively used by fishermen. As we

round a slight bend the bottom set of three locks of the lower Wilmcote flight comes into view. Here the canal slowly climbs the incline from the Avon valley. Across the fields, to the right, the railway parallels the canal.

A forlorn lock cottage stands beside the top lock. From this lock

On the Wilmcote flight

we can look back at the rooftops of Stratford, above the trees, down in the valley below. Ahead we can see the first of the split bridges which were used on this canal. The split allowed the towrope to pass through, as there was no room for a towpath beneath. Beyond the bridge is another lock, this time in a wooded area. The canal continues to climb and soon we reach a flight of another three locks. The canal here is like a country lane, with a hedge on either side and fields beyond. The towpath is rutted, but still offers a passable route.

By the side of the upper of these three locks lies another white-painted rectangular lock cottage and, beyond, the canal starts to move into a shallow cutting. The towpath rides along the top of the bank and becomes almost cut off from the canal. We pass another split bridge and continue along an overgrown and uneven path.

After a while we reach Wilmcote, the site of the bridge that nearly caused the complete closure of the canal in 1958, when Warwickshire County Council sought abandonment. Beyond the bridge lies a popular mooring for boats. Past these moorings the towpath becomes bumpy, but is right in the midst of the countryside.

For the next mile the canal meanders through undulating countryside and the towpath is, in places, completely overgrown. Along this reach, only one decrepit and overgrown split bridge is passed. The canal follows a contour line, with the land sloping off to the right.

Once we reach split bridge No. 57, the canal starts to come on to an embankment. On the left a row of cottages shows where an old wharf used to be. Ahead lies the narrow section of Edstone Aqueduct, one of the wonders of the canal. Its length of 475 feet makes it the second longest cast-iron canal aqueduct in the country. The towpath runs beside the trough at base level and is edged by an ornate balustrade. The whole structure is quite remarkable, and is carried on thirteen tapering brick piers, each over 20 feet in height and capped with dressed stone. It is well worth spending time to explore this unique structure. Beyond the aqueduct the canal at first rides along a straight embankment and, when it reaches the valley side, the single 'Odd Lock' lifts the canal to the next long reach. Along this section, the canal cuts through the higher ground of the former Forest of Arden. Although the original forest has long since gone, the deep cuttings are still overgrown with bushes, which often extend to the water's edge. After about a quarter of a mile, at bridge No. 55, the towpath crosses to the left bank. For a way the walking is difficult, but soon improves – only to deteriorate again. After a while the rooftops of Wootton Wawen can be seen and we reach another, shorter, iron-troughed aqueduct which conveys the canal over the main Birmingham road, on which is situated the Navigation Inn. Beyond the aqueduct is a large basin area, now a hire base for Anglo-Welsh Cruisers.

The next reach, of about a mile, passes through some very pleasant farmland. Some sections of the canal are wooded; beyond, the meadows roll over the low hills. Farms are dotted about and, in places, the fields are linked by bridges in various states of repair, and often overgrown.

At Preston Bagot, various road bridges cross the canal. Below them boats moor to allow the crews to go to the Crab Mill Inn, a short distance up the main road. At bridge No. 48 the towpath crosses to the right bank, but it is easier to make a slight detour past the Manor House, to join the canal at bridge No. 47, where a gate offers access to the lockside. Just above the lock, on the right, is the Haven Tea Room. Beyond this, the towpath leads on to the neat lock No. 37 with its splendid lock cottage. This barrel-roofed building is one of six which are a unique feature of the next section of the canal. All are in various states of modification and repair.

At first the canal continues in a wooded reach until lock No. 33 is reached with its split bridge. Here the towpath moves to the right-hand bank and is at first in quite good condition – if uneven. After about half a mile lock No. 32 is reached and we continue towards Lowsonford, the towpath side offering some boats a permanent base. The canal soon bears to the right, where an old red-brick arched bridge crosses the canal. Beyond this bridge, and to the right of the lock, is perhaps the most rustic of all the barrel-roofed cottages, still in almost its original state. Beyond and on the opposite bank is the Fleur de Lys Inn.

From Lowsonford the towpath becomes a well-used path all the way to Kingswood Junction. The canal slowly rises through ten more locks, spaced at regular intervals. The whole of this length makes a pleasant 2-mile walk. Just below lock No. 28 is another barrel-roofed cottage, this time at right-angles to the canal. Here hand-painted canal ware is sold.

After another short reach passing the remaining four locks we come near Kingswood Junction, where a colourful array of residential craft line the towpath edge. Rounding a bend, and above lock No. 22, the National Trust canal maintenance yard comes into view. The canal yard lies adjacent to lock No. 21. It is an

The barrel-roofed lock cottage at Lowsonford. The roof was made out of a wooden frame originally used to support the canal bridges during reconstruction – an ingenious method of recycling large-scale waste!

exceptionally good example of a modern maintenance depot and provides ready access. The old yard buildings make an attractive sight, with the red and blue brick buildings contrasting with the tarred wood of the Toll Office. A split bridge takes the towpath over the entrance to the canal. Looking northwards from it one can see the first locks of the Northern Section of the canal rising ahead. To the right lies the shallow lock and short link channel leading to the Grand Union Canal. In between the two lies an array of small reservoirs, which provide a venue for anglers. Our exploration ends here.

Those who complete the full 13-mile walk will have realized the problems that beset the National Trust in maintaining the canal: poor access, decayed structures and lack of finance to employ additional staff all take their toll. Even so, it is a unique rural waterway and deserves far more loving attention than it presently receives.

Further reading

Charles Hadfield and John Norris, *Waterways to Stratford*. David and Charles, 1968.

Guy Johnson, *Save the Stratford Canal*. David and Charles, 1983.

Stratford-upon-Avon (Southern Section) Canal Guide, National Trust.

'Town Trail', Stratford-upon-Avon Town Council.

The Birmingham Canal Navigations

from Gas Street Basin (SP 062867) via Farmers Bridge Junction, Icknield Square Junction, Smethwick Junction and Smethwick Locks, along the Old Main Line to Spon Lane Locks and Oldbury, Bromford Lane (SP 994903)
Map 139

In its heyday the Birmingham Navigations system was well over 160 miles in length and even today over 100 miles are navigable. This concentration of canals is surprising when one considers that Birmingham lies on a high plateau in an area ill served with rivers. However, the variety of mines and limestone quarries prompted the growth of man-made navigations, which in turn attracted an extensive concentration of heavy industry along their banks. As a result more than 550 private basins were developed, together with an array of railway interchange facilities, maintenance yards and ancillary structures. Water supply for 212 narrow locks was always a problem, and as a result various reservoirs and supply feeders were combined with pumping stations to meet the heavy traffic demands. Today there is minimal commercial movement, restricted to single waste boats, a far cry from the 1880s when some eight million tons of goods were carried annually. The change results from the movement of industry away from the canals and the decline of local mines. Derelict land, decaying factories, and urban redevelopment schemes are now sad reminders of the glories of the past. Even so, the elements that survive offer a strange attraction of their own. The cast-iron bollards and signs, neat overbridges and functional lock gear, worn stonework and rope cuts in the brick-work – all recall the heavy traffic and past prosperity of these canals.

Today pleasure craft move through the locks, while cyclists and walkers plod the towpaths which were once the domain of the horse. The Birmingham canals were formerly the artery for the city's trade; today they provide 'green fingers' through the urban sprawl, offering a surprisingly peaceful and almost rural setting, which never ceases to amaze people who stumble upon these watery roads that stretch out like an untidy spider's web from the very heart of the city centre itself.

Our exploration seeks to impart a feeling for the Birmingham Canal Navigations and at the same time include some of the most historic features. It also aims to provide a contrast between the old and the new. The walk includes the first canal in Birmingham, built to James Brindley's design, opened between Easy Row Wharf in central Birmingham (by Navigation Street) and Wednesbury in 1769, and subsequently linked to the Staffordshire and Worcestershire Canal at Aldersley Junction, just north of Wolverhampton, in 1772. This was a typical contour canal and avoided all deep cuttings and embankments by the use of circuits round hills or locks. As a result it took 22 miles to cover the 13 miles, as the crow flies, to Wolverhampton. Originally two separate flights of six locks were needed to raise the canal over the hill in between at Smethwick, where a reservoir, feeder and pump were required to provide an adequate water supply. The excessive lockage caused so much delay that, only twenty-one years after it was opened, John Smeaton was employed to build a lower summit level, by means of a cutting, to save three locks at either side. He also built a parallel flight of locks at the Birmingham end to facilitate increased traffic flow. At the dawn of the railway era the Birmingham Navigations Company decided that it must modernize to compete, and commissioned Thomas Telford to design further improvements to the Main Line and so speed up the traffic. His scheme was similar to the motorway today; the distance from Birmingham to Aldersley was reduced by 7 miles. This 'straight' canal, 40 feet wide with a double towing path, in up to 70-foot-deep cuttings, with spectacular bridges, provided the optimum route with little to hinder the ever-increasing flow of traffic between the mines and works. Over the passage of the past 150 years, commercial traffic has disappeared, but the functional structures remain. It is their splendour that we plan to explore.

The original wharf of the Birmingham Canal, near Easy Row, has become the site of the new television centre, so we now have to take another turning off Broad Street by a side road named Gas Street. A small arched entrance leads into the originally secretive and once secluded canal basin. However, the demolition of the warehouses of the Severn & Canal Carrying Company in 1976 has completely altered the scene. Now a cleared site immediately takes the eye, while the tall modern television centre dominates the horizon and narrow boats moor on either side of the Worcester Bar. Originally inter-company rivalry meant that goods had to be trans-shipped across the stone bar. It was not until 1815 that the stop lock, which lies below our entry point, made a physical union between the two canals possible. Boats now pass freely, and residents have to cross the lock by a small removable bridge to reach their craft.

We turn left and pass under Broad Street tunnel, beyond which the canal is enclosed between high brick walls. High on the right a series of red-painted trapdoors allows fire hoses access to the water below. Further along, the old brewmaster's house is currently being restored. Elsewhere, derelict buildings and old workshops lie sad and forlorn, waiting for new ideas and new life. Ahead lies a canal junction, complete with an island roundabout on which a signpost defines: 'Worcester 30 miles/ Wolverhampton 13 miles'. Beyond the island, a neat black-and-white painted Horsley Ironworks bridge, built in 1827, carries a towpath over the route which leads to Farmers Bridge and the award-winning Cambrian Wharf redevelopment area.

We turn left and over another canal, the Oozell's Street loop. From this bridge, to the right we gain an impressive view of Birmingham as it stretches out below. Turning westwards, we can see the start of Telford's New Main Line, which is also crossed by a neat level bridge that links our path to the towpath on the right bank. Although the Telford line has a towpath on each bank, we cross here to the right-hand side and continue westwards.

The scene is dominated by site clearance work underway on either bank. Old factories rapidly disappear and open sites are left. Our route soon passes under the first of the sturdy twin blue-brick arched bridges that span the wide canal. Here again, firemen's hatches can be seen. About 100 yards beyond this bridge, the Oozell's Street loop re-emerges from the left from beneath a cast-iron towpath bridge. Soon we pass under St Vincent Street bridge, where a new gate and earth slope offer a link to the road. Beyond this bridge new council flats line the right bank; factories dominate the left bank, none using the services that the canal could still provide.

Our towpath soon rises to cross an old basin arm, now unused, and the railway beyond begins to run alongside the canal on the right. Our route now passes under Monument Road bridge. Looking ahead, we can begin to appreciate the true significance

A little to the west of the Soho loop

of the wide straight nineteenth-century equivalent of a motorway that Telford built.

Just past Monument Road bridge, on the left, another section of the 'old' Brindley line leaves on the left. This is the Icknield Port loop, which also serves as a water supply feeder, bringing water from the Rotton Park reservoir that lies at its head, adjacent to the British Waterways Board depot. As there is no continuous towpath around the loop, to see the complete line we have to make a brief detour to Icknield Port Road, which offers a view over the depot to the reservoir embankment beyond.

Our route continues along the Telford line, which is rejoined after only a short distance by the returning arm of the Icknield Port loop. On this occasion the old Brindley line cuts across our path, at right-angles, and immediately enters the Soho loop, which leaves the 'new' line to the right. Black and white painted bridges cross both the loop entrances and another bridge crosses the new line just beyond.

At this point we have the choice of following the towpath of the Soho loop, or continuing along the Telford Main Line. The easier course is to continue forward past the unique canal cross-roads and follow the New Main Line, which quickly begins to cut through slightly higher land on either bank. On the right, the railway slowly rises to take a higher course. A single brick pier in the centre of the canal ahead remains as a sad monument to the former Chad Valley branch line, which originally crossed the canal at this point.

Ahead, the cutting through which the canal passes grows deeper, and is spanned by the wide blue-brick skew span of Lee Bridge. Beyond this bridge the canal stretches out in a long straight course, the banks covered with dandelions. It soon passes under Winson Green Bridge, again of a brick skew arched design.

Sans paroles. *Soho*

Along here both sides of the canal are lined with huge sandstone blocks which blend in with the drab colours that surround them. Under the bridge the towpath is brick-paved with a regular series of lines of bricks on edge, offering the tow horses a better grip.

The grassy banks of the cutting ahead almost create the image of a rural canal, but an estate of new houses and the factory chimneys on the skyline destroy the illusion. The towpath soon rises to cross the returning course of the Soho loop. Underfoot, the structure of cast-iron panels and the way they are bolted together can be readily seen, because the upper surface of the path has eroded. Ahead, one of the former toll islands now lies derelict in the centre of the canal. The original octagonal toll booth has long since been removed, and the island now acts as an unofficial rubbish dump. On the right bank a railway yard soon dominates. The earth embankment on the left originally provided access to the Cape Arm, another loop of the Brindley canal, which has been filled in. The point where the Arm used to return can still be identified further on, by a bricked-up bridge on the left, just before the end of the long straight reach.

Just after the former Cape Arm junction, the canal gently curves to pass under the railway, and then is hemmed in by industry on either bank. Beyond the railway bridge a girder bridge, attached to the railway span, offers access to the opposite bank. The route ahead offers a true image of what the uninitiated all expect Birmingham to look like. Factory chimneys and extractor fans belch fumes into the air and buildings are discoloured by thick layers of dust. However, even here the canal side is still lined with dandelions and ferns, which manage to grow alongside the factory walls. We quickly pass another cleared factory site, a steel works on the right, and under the span of Rathbone Bridge. Some way ahead is a black Horseley Ironworks roving bridge, and here the canal divides. Telford's Main Line continues to the left – we branch off to the right, along the old Brindley line. Our path leads forward up a brick-paved slope to the road over Rolfe Bridge, which we cross diagonally to join the towpath on the left of the remaining lock above the bridge. On the right of the bridge is the Old Navigation public house.

Rope-wear on a cast-iron bridge rail

Above Rolfe Bridge the area between the old and new canal lines has been designated as the site of some landscaping work, through a Community Task Force project, in a scheme to create

Writing on the wall. Muntz's solid-drawn brass works is long since gone. The decorated railway bridge is nearby

the Galton Valley Canal Park. Above the lock the canal curves to the left, and soon the second of the three remaining Smethwick Locks comes into view. Here the canal water is a strange green colour, no doubt due to pollution from one of the factories alongside the line.

A small bridge precedes the third and top lock of the flight, and by crossing over it we can still find some traces of the original Brindley Lock chamber, which was duplicated at the time Smeaton improved the line. All the original Brindley locks on the far side were demolished many years ago – only the top lock entrance area still remains. Beyond this lock the old and new lines come close to each other, but our towpath rises to cross an arm that, surprisingly, leaves to the left. This is the Engine Arm, which is carried over the lower Telford line by a beautiful cast-iron aqueduct built in 1825 – the amazing thing is that the large end piers are made of stone, painted black. The original Boulton and Watt pumping engine near this point has since been removed, and is now in the Birmingham Museum of Science and Industry. All the water needed for the old line summit level is now supplied from Titford Pools, along a $2\frac{1}{2}$-mile feeder which enters through an inlet at the terminus of the Engine Arm. It can be seen by following the towpath on the left-hand bank of the Arm over the aqueduct and through the factories.

Our route continues westwards along the left bank of the lowered Smeaton summit level. We cross over a weir, and the canal soon curves under Brasshouse Bridge. Where this bridge spans the Telford line, there is a spectacular high blue-brick arched bridge. The view westwards from Brasshouse Bridge makes the detour to the road level well worth while. One can see the dynamic style of Telford's deep cutting on the left, contrasted with the higher Smeaton's line, which lies beyond the large brick-built pumphouse that separates the two. Higher still, on the right embankment, we can just make out the level of the earlier Brindley line, which climbed up a further three locks here to clear the top of Smethwick Hill. A pathway leads off from the left side and northern end of Brasshouse Bridge, and for part of its route follows the line of the old Brindley canal.

Our path continues along the left bank of the higher Smeaton line, past Smethwick pumphouse. Soon we reach the point where the two canals move apart, and by looking up to the right it is easy to identify the level of the former Brindley line by a narrow ridge that runs along the bank above. Walking forward, we find ourselves in a shaded reach; only the rooftops on our right remind us that we are in the midst of suburban Birmingham.

Rounding a bend, the new summit tunnel confronts us, its white semicircular concrete entrance arch looking quite out of place. Fortunately, a wide towpath passes through the new tunnel, protected with a railing at the water's side. After the tunnel, our route passes under two high bridges.

Soon the skyline is dominated by high-rise flats. Below them a motorway crosses the canal on its own huge concrete track, supported by thick round piles that grow from the very sides of the canal; here the canal has been slightly realigned to fit the motorway path. Soon the canal manages to gain the daylight again, but the towpath remains under the motorway bridge edge. To the left a barren strip of land under the arches is devoid of life, an indication of the blight the motorway brings. After about 100 yards, the canal manages to escape to the left, and for a while defends its own path. Ahead, a small brick arched bridge crosses the canal. We pass a small wharf area and continue on under this bridge. The canal is forced to continue its route beneath the motorway span. Soon a lock takes a branch of the canal away to the right. This is the top lock of the Spon Lane flight, reputed to be the oldest working flight of locks in the country. To approach it we need to cross the canal on the Wolverhampton side of Spon Lane bridge; however, before doing so, it is worth while making a short detour to see the Stewart Aqueduct, which crosses the Telford main line about 200 yards ahead and is approached by continuing along the towpath on the left. Some steps spiral down to the left to the Telford line below. If you make the effort to walk down them you will get an impression of the size and massive strength of the aqueduct. Beyond, some of the concrete piers for the motorway now stubbornly rise from the middle of the Telford line. High on the left, a railway runs parallel to the canal. At this one spot we see the coming together of the three modes of transport – canal, road and rail – with the bonus of the canal flyover as well!

Having studied the complex, we return via Spon Lane bridge to Spon Lane Locks. The top lock lowers the Smeaton line down towards Wolverhampton. At the far end of this lock an old split bridge is in a sorry state, but the lock still works. From the top lock, the canal runs in a straight line down to the newer Telford line, some 20 feet below, passing through two further locks. The towpath, a wide, grassy band, provides an excellent route for joggers. Passing under a rusty Bailey bridge we reach the second of the three locks. The bottom lock of the three proved to be in fine condition, with one gate proudly supporting a plaque reading: 'Built Bradley 1981'!

Smethwick bottom lock

Below the lock, the old and new lines unite. Two neatly painted Horseley Ironworks cast-iron bridges cross the canals to allow the towpaths to interlink. In between, another toll island stands forlorn in the middle of the canal. Our route takes us over the second bridge to follow the grassy towpath westwards along the left bank. Soon, on both the left and right banks, a variety of works and yards dominates the view, and the canal offers a peaceful path through the hubbub beyond. After passing a steel-yard on the left, a ramp offers access to Bromford Lane, which crosses the canal. If we turn left here a short walk brings us to Oldbury Station, for a speedy return to central Birmingham.

For those who want to walk further, retrace the route by walking back along the south bank of the Telford line: it is quite startling to compare the differences between the two levels. Even along those stretches of common route it is surprising how different everything looks from the opposite direction!

Further reading

H.R.G. Beavon, *Along the Birmingham Canals – A Boating and Walking Guide*. Tetradon, 1981.

S.R. Broadbridge, *The Birmingham Canal Navigations, Volume 1, 1768–1846*. David and Charles, 1974.

P. Groves, *The Navigation Way. A hundred mile towpath walk around Birmingham and the West Midlands*. Tetradon, 1982.

The Staffordshire and Worcestershire Canal

from the River Severn at Stourport (SO 810710) via the Town Basin and northwards to Kidderminster Town Lock (SO 829767)
Maps 138 and 139

The Staffordshire and Worcestershire Canal southern section is known locally as the 'Stour Cut', and is one of the best examples of the work of the great canal pioneer, James Brindley, for it provided the River Severn link in his 'Grand Cross' scheme for connecting the ports of Liverpool, Hull, London and Bristol by artificial waterways. The Act of Parliament for the Staffordshire and Worcestershire Canal was passed in May 1766. Brindley was responsible for setting out the line and, in consequence, for most of its route the canal follows the contours and hugs valley sides. The choice of the exact location of its junction with the Severn was mainly decided by engineering constraints; Bewdley was the natural contender, since it was an established river port. However, a sandstone shelf which followed the 100-foot contour on the right wall of the Stour valley offered an ideal track for a Brindley canal; it also avoided the swampy valley floor. This resulted in the selection of a site about 100 yards above the Stour confluence. The Staffordshire and Worcestershire Canal Company envisaged the construction of a small Severnside terminal port, and originally chose the name Stourmouth, which was changed to Newport before the choice of Stourport was made in 1771.

Initially the Canal Company purchased only the minimum area of land necessary for its plans. Two Severnside fields, together a little over 7 acres, were developed as the site of a single terminal basin, linked to the River Severn by two locks, separated by a small intermediate basin above the flood plain. Quays were levelled around the dock perimeter and two small graving docks were built for Severn trows locking up into the intermediate basin. The amount of traffic that flocked to the dock in 1771 exceeded all expectations, and by 1773 plans were being made to purchase more land to build a second basin, together with another river connection. The Long Warehouse was erected on the eastern side of the dock, and the whole of the southern edge was taken up by the Iron Warehouse and an extension shed. Apart from these dockside structures the site was relatively bare, and as a result the company had to build cottages for lock keepers, the wharfinger and other employees. To provide for visitors and other higher grades of employees, the company erected a large hotel, the Tontine, which overlooked the riverbank. This great structure was completed in 1773, and the following year a 'chaise house' was erected close by. A garden was laid out on land sloping towards the river, in an effort to command the waterfront and impress on even the most hardened waterman that the new port was the place to trade

The flow of traffic quickly grew and by 1795 at least nine warehouses graced the two large basins. In 1804 a plan was drawn up for a third basin, which was to have a separate upper canal lock and a lateral link with the original upper basin. Unfortunately only the lateral cut was made, leaving the new basin as a cul-de-sac. Beyond the dock boundary, the town of Stourport rapidly moulded itself around the dock estate and by 1795 had a population of 1,300 people, a far cry from the dozen local inhabitants in 1760! By 1820 Stourport had become a complete town, and a contemporary writer described it thus: 'Its houses . . . mostly on a good scale, its street comfortable, full of shops and thronged with people; whilst an air even of elegance pervades it'. This period of maximum prosperity was unfortunately short-lived, and with the opening of the Birmingham to Gloucester Railway in 1840 the demise of the canal soon followed. The massive Tontine was subdivided, and by 1842 contained twenty separate dwellings besides the original inn. A slight reprieve was gained when the Kidderminster carpet and worsted industry spread to the town. However this trade far from compensated for the traffic which was lost because of the deterioration of the lower Severn Navigation. In fact it was the success of the Kidderminster and Stourport Electric Tramway, completed in 1898, that brought new life to the town, offering easy access to riverine Stourport for Midlands holidaymakers. Soon a bandstand and a promenade graced the waterfront, and a semi-permanent fairground took the place of some lower wharves.

After two centuries as a canal port, the Stourport dockland has now totally reverted to its originally minor role as a resort. The New Basin has been filled in to serve as a timber yard, and both the Tontine and the remaining warehouses have been converted into flats. The main basin is now a mooring for pleasure craft, while the riverside quays are the starting point for boat trips.

We start our walk by the River Severn. The two entrances to the canal are east of the Severn Bridge, beyond Crown Basin and its adjacent fairground. Access to the locks is gained by walking eastwards along the riverside path and over the swing bridge, at the entrance of Crown Basin, from which the path continues to a humpback bridge that spans the entrance to the narrow lock. This is the lock for the canal and above it, in a staircase, a second lock lifts canal boats to the Bottom or Lower Basin. On the left of the basin, parallel to the second lock, is a covered dry dock. Two further staircase narrow locks lift craft from the Bottom Basin to the Clock Basin, which lies to the west of the Clock Warehouse.

Our path continues eastwards to the Barge or Trow Lock. It is interesting to compare both the size and the lift of the two different locks: the former is less than half the width of the second, and provides half the lift. Our path crosses this wide lock from which, looking northwards, we can get an impressive view of the Tontine. It is worth continuing on to the riverbank downstream of the Barge Lock entrance; this whole area forms the public quay, and its stone wharf extends for about 100 yards.

We now go to the left of the Tontine. Ahead on the left is the Motor Yacht Club House, situated in one of the original warehouses. On the bar between the Clock Basin and the Upper Basin is a dominant clock tower, built by Samuel Thorpe in 1812. In between is a lock house beside the barge entrance to the Upper Basin. Our path turns right along the basin edge, and links with Mart Lane, along which we turn to the left. A viewing area has recently been constructed on the left, by the basin edge – an ideal point from which to watch the craft in the basin and see the full splendour of the Clock Warehouse beyond. Looking north from this spot we can see the entrance to the Staffordshire and Worcestershire Canal, as it tucks under the low York Street bridge. Alongside the basin is a wharf with its own crane; a fine old warehouse has been converted into a boat chandlery.

Our route crosses York Street to the pavement alongside the York Street lock wall. The canal here is at road level and the lock lowers craft some 12 feet to enable them to pass under the tiny Wallfield Bridge into the basin beyond. Situated at either end of the lock are two old mid-nineteenth-century toll cottages. Further along, on the left, the Dartline Hire Boat yard is based around the former York Street canal maintenance yard wharf.

A gate beside York Street Lock offers access to the towpath, which passes beyond an old warehouse to pass under Lower Mitton Bridge. Along the next reach the canal takes a straight path beside backs of buildings, gardens and yards, but soon gains a hedgerow on its right, with derelict buildings along the left bank, then swings to the right. Alongside this curve lies an old warehouse with a long integral wharf area to the canal level. Fluted metal pillars, each with its own arch, support the solid structure.

The canal passes under Gilgal Bridge. The route acquires a green backdrop, with a variety of trees on the sloping left bank leaning out over the canal. A hedge on the towpath side continues to protect the walker from the noise of the traffic beyond. The towpath crosses an old wharf area – now grassed – with a gate leading out to the road which, at this point, lies below the canal.

The canal soon bends sharply northwards as it reaches the edge of the Stour valley. The canal engineers carefully chose the course above the flood plain on an easily worked sandstone ledge. This is especially evident at the corner on the left-hand bank, which has an almost cliff-like profile as it rises up to a churchyard above, where we can see the gravestones and memorials, all overgrown. A pedestrian bridge crosses the canal on the bend, and slopes down at an alarming angle. It links the churchyard to the towpath and a path to the Stour valley below.

From here the canal heads northwards, with the towpath bank dropping sharply down to the right. The path along this reach is well used. The towpath soon passes close beside some cottages, which were built by the Canal Company in 1800. Beyond them the Bird in Hand has an adjacent wharf, where boat crews still moor their craft.

The canal now passes under the wide brick arch that once carried the Severn Valley line over the canal. Beyond the bridge, to the left, are the remains of the former railway and canal interchange basin, now overgrown; it is the only basin of this sort along the whole canal. A little way along the wharf, an old toll cottage now lies derelict. Just north of the railway bridge, on the towpath edge, is a pulley wheel that was used to assist boats in and out of the basin. The canal here is wide and acted as a lay-by for craft using the wharf.

The towpath continues as a well used path, although the grass is high on either edge. After a while we reach Upper Mitton Bridge. Upper Mitton was one of the two villages that merged to become Stourport when the canal was built. Beyond the bridge, the canal clings closely to the valley side. Looking to the right, the River Stour sweeps across the valley floor in a wide arc, soon almost reaching the bottom of the steep towpath bank. For a short distance the canal crosses an embankment before entering a slight cutting near the site of a public wharf for the villagers of Upper Mitton. From the wharf the left bank rises sharply, with terraces of houses, each climbing one above the other.

To the right, the River Stour reaches all the way up to the base of the towpath bank, and a spill weir provides an overflow from the canal. Because the towpath is so high above the river here, it offers the ideal vantage point.

Along the next reach, huge walnut trees grow on the towpath side, rising high above the neatly trimmed hedge. In some places the older hedgerow has been replaced with new thorn bushes to fill the gaps. After a while the canal bank to the left becomes wooded again, with tall oak trees and silver birches interspersed with the odd May bush and even an apple tree here and there. In a couple of places pathways through the trees lead down to the canal, to provide watering points. A rusted sluice gear at the towpath edge allows water to be drained off from the canal into the drainage duct that parallels the towpath embankment. Low sandstone cliffs now begin to dominate the canal bank. Ahead is Oldington Bridge, one of the original Brindley-designed structures, with walls of red brick and a sandstone block stringer course and coping. A farm track crosses here and extends out into the valley floor beyond. The remains of a derelict wharf can be seen just past the bridge.

Beyond the bridge we soon reach the remains of a former cottage on the towpath side. Ahead lies a towpath bridge which carries the towpath over an arm. The canal widens here to provide a turning space. Alongside the arm, with its derelict lock now completely overgrown, are the foundations of an old lock keeper's cottage, demolished in the distant past. The rubble still remains, hidden under the weeds. A bridge nameplate on the outer arch states 'Platts Wharf'. The site, however, was originally 'Pratt's' Wharf; it would seem that an error on an early large-scale Ordnance Survey map has been perpetuated ever since. The derelict lock was built around 1850 to link the canal to a

Falling Sands Bridge, and the viaduct now owned by the Severn Valley Railway Company

section of the River Stour, which was made navigable as far as the Wilden Iron Works. Before the lock was built, goods were trans-shipped at Pratt's Wharf into smaller river boats. The lock was last used in 1949 and has fallen derelict. The Wilden Iron Works downstream closed a couple of years later, and the river navigation was allowed to revert to its pre-navigation level. A footpath still follows the old river navigation's banks and it should be possible to complete a circuit back to Oldington Bridge, if one has the time.

Our walk continues northwards. Soon a pipeline crosses the canal, this time on its own girder bridge; it then promptly tunnels underground on the right, through the marshy land with drainage ditches lined with celandines and interspersed with willow trees. Soon the woods grow thicker on both banks and the canal curves to reach a lock, with tall trees on the left bank coming right down to the lock side. The lock site is in a picturesque setting with a sandy bank to the left and drifts of bluebells under the trees. A wrought-iron bridge crosses the front of the lock gates, offering access to the woods. The site is easily associated with its name, Falling Sands Lock.

After the lock, the canal follows a contour path, the river coming quite close to the towpath edge. As we approach Kidderminster the canal curves and is crossed by a high seven-arched railway viaduct some way ahead, preceded by a bridge. The viaduct carries the Severn valley linkline over the canal. Enthusiasts have already reopened the section between Bewdley and Bridgnorth, and have recently rebuilt the link through to Kidderminster. Again the view of the canal bridge ahead – Falling Sands Bridge – is marred by pipes that cross in front of it.

Some way further on a lock is carved out of the sandstone ledge, which is especially marked above the lock chambers: this is Caldwall Lock. A split bridge precedes the lock, with neat railings and sandstone abutments. An impressive sandstone cliff rises behind the lock. By the lock side we still can see where an old lock cottage stood. To the right, beyond the lock, factories begin to dominate the valley floor across the river, which remains close to the canal side.

Our route continues northwards: after passing under a modern road bridge the remains of Old Foundry Wharf are in evidence to the left, and further along Roundhill Coal Wharf lies disused, with large trees growing around the site. For a while the river remains close to the canal, but soon swings off to the right through the mass of factories that seem to fill the valley floor. The canal manages to maintain a straighter path and soon passes under another bridge by another old wharf, now converted to a lorry yard. The towpath dives underneath a metal girder bridge and beyond it lies the former Kidderminster Public Wharf, now disused. A high wall lines the towpath on the right, behind which is one of the many Kidderminster carpet factories. Ahead a large gasholder dominates the skyline, while next to the canal stands a fine factory chimney made from yellow and blue bricks, with the corners lined alternately with bricks of red and blue. The canal now becomes more derelict, with the high walls of old factories left ragged where they have been demolished. In places, on the left bank, renovated cottages back on to the canal. Just opposite a timber yard the towpath rises to cross a factory arm, now filled in. Our route continues onwards, up and over another infilled arm, which was the former coal wharf entrance to the gasworks.

At this point we are near the centre of Kidderminster, where extensive road construction work blocked my path through to the lock beyond and forced a detour, though I was assured by the contractors that the towpath route will be preserved, once the construction works have been completed.

Just above the Town Lock, the canal passes over an aqueduct which allows the River Stour to pass under the canal line. It is difficult to get a good view of this low three-arched structure from the lock side, but we can see the river rushing below. Our walk ends here, right in the centre of Kidderminster, a town which once brought much trade to the canal and also prospered from the wares that were shipped out from the many wharfs and arms. Now the town has turned its back on the waterway. The only attractive spot is the little wharf in the lee of St Mary's church. One can only hope that, as other redevelopment plans evolve, more thought will be given to the future role of the canal that once served this town so well.

Further reading

C. Hadfield, *Canals of the West Midlands*. David and Charles, 1969.

J. Ian Langford, Towpath Guide No. 1 – 'Staffordshire and Worcestershire Canal'. Goose and Son, 1974.

The Droitwich Canals

from the junction with the Worcester and Birmingham Canal near Hanbury Wharf (SO 923629) via Droitwich, Salwarpe, Ladywood, Porters Mill and on to Hawford and the River Severn junction (SO 842609)
Map 150

The Droitwich Canals and the prosperity of the town of Droitwich have often been interlinked. From the earliest times, man has known of the wild brine streams which bubble to the surface in the Salwarpe Valley. The Romans were quick to exploit the salt and developed a system of salt ways to transport it. The salt was produced by evaporating the brine on site, but the major difficulty was always transport. Pack horses and later bullock carts were used to move the salt to the markets, but never with great success. Worcester, on the River Severn, offered the best potential outlet. The problem was reaching the town with the load intact. By the Middle Ages, local merchants had turned their attention to the River Salwarpe. However, it was not until Andrew Yarranton was called in during 1655 that any attempt was made to get navigation works built. Lord Windsor was subsequently involved in building Flash Locks, but even these did not last very long and ultimately were washed away.

The idea of creating a canal to link Droitwich to the Severn resulted in the employment of James Brindley in 1768 to construct an artificial navigation down the Salwarpe valley. He employed John Priddey as resident engineer, and in 1771 the $6\frac{3}{4}$-mile-long Droitwich Barge Canal was opened. Eight locks enabled the 20-ton cargoes to pass from the town salt wharf to the River Severn beyond. Coal was brought up the canal to fuel the works. Subsequently local agricultural produce from the valley was carried from mill wharfs along the line. By 1780 heavy traffic was making the canal a huge financial success, but clouds loomed on the horizon when in 1789 the Worcester and Birmingham Canal was mooted. Fortunately, under an Act of 1791, subsidy arrangements were agreed to compensate for loss of trade. The Worcester and Birmingham Canal was finally completed in 1815 and thereafter paid dearly for this subsidy commitment. The coming of the railways and the opening of Stoke Salt Works, away from the town, further diminished the competitive position of the town and its canal. As a result the Droitwich Junction Canal was opened in 1854 to provide Droitwich with a direct link to the industry of Birmingham, via the Worcester and Birmingham Canal. The Barge Locks were extended at this time. Subsequently canals were taken over by the Sharpness New Docks Company in 1864, when the Droitwich Barge Canal was improved substantially, and built to a deeper gauge, in a last-ditch effort to boost its trade. However, the combination of railway, and later road, competition and the demise of the town's salt industry finally took its toll. The Barge Canal carried its last commercial traffic, a boatload of hay, in 1918 and the Junction Canal survived until the mid-1920s before it also fell into disuse. The inevitable consequence was that both canals were abandoned under an Act of July 1939, and both waterways became tracts of land in the ownership of Droitwich Borough Council.

In the post-war era, Droitwich's fortunes revived when the area was selected as a site for a 'new town'. One of the features of the development was the use of the Salwarpe valley floor as the focus for recreation and open space. Just as the fortunes of Droitwich town revived, so did those of the canal. In 1973 the local authorities and the Inland Waterways Association promoted the formation of the Droitwich Canals Trust. Since that time the Trust has been raising funds and undertaking remedial work on the Droitwich Barge Canal with the ultimate aim of reopening it as a through navigation. Hopefully the Droitwich Junction Canal too will be restored at some stage.

Our exploration covers both canals and provides the opportunity to see the various states of decay and repair. More particularly it provides an interesting walk along part of a Roman salt way and on down the Salwarpe valley to the River Severn. What better place to start our walk than a pub! The old salt way (B 4090) now crosses the Worcester and Birmingham Canal at Hanbury Wharf, where the Eagle and Sun stands on the eastern canal bank. Looking to the north from the canal bridge, we can just make out the blocked-off and reed-filled entrance to the Droitwich Junction Canal on the left bank. An access road crosses over the Droitwich Junction Canal line nearby. In the early spring or late autumn, when the weeds have died back, it is possible to trace the start of the Junction Canal and, to the west, find the remains of the flight of three deep narrowlock chambers, as they make a gentle staircase down the hill on the right of the salt way. It is fascinating to find the decayed remains of the lock gates, and see the blue railway brick lock chambers, in a reasonable state of repair.

After exploring the Hanbury Wharf complex, we set off westwards downhill along the salt way. Our route continues westwards along the B4090 road, passing under the new motorway bridge, beyond which, on the right, is a concrete driveway that leads northwards up to Impney Farm. About 100 yards along this drive we can trace the filled-in remains of an old railway brick-arched bridge that crossed over the former line of the canal. Body Brook runs alongside the old canal line here, and the restorers plan to use the line of the brook to recreate their link under the motorway through to the Worcester and Birmingham Canal.

We return to the old salt way, which soon bends to reach a line of chestnut trees. After a while the dry line of the former canal route passes behind a petrol station, to the right, and just west of the fenced area beyond, and opposite No. 27, a little alleyway with a brick wall on the left allows access to the remains of the waterway. Here we can see the patched relics of some sluices, which divert the water into the river alongside, as the canal line itself is infilled beyond this point. Our route continues westwards along the B4090, past an old toll lodge, on the left, at the junction with the Tibberton road, and on to the main crossroads beyond. Here we cross the A38 and turn northwards for a short way to reach Chapel Bridge, which spans the River Salwarpe. At this point the river was used as the route of the Junction Canal. We can gain access to the towpath by taking an unofficial short cut through the edge of a garage forecourt and down the river bank. By turning east under Chapel Bridge we can walk a few yards to the point at which the Junction Canal and the River Salwarpe join. Beyond this, it is possible to trace the line of the Junction Canal for a few more yards before it disappears into a bricked-up bridge. We now have to retrace our steps under the ornate ironwork of Chapel Bridge, and follow the southern bank of the Salwarpe for some 50 yards to the Barge Lock, which lies left of the river.

The Barge Lock, with its complex set of gate alcoves to allow for different river levels, has recently been re-excavated by the Droitwich Canals Trust. This is the start of the Barge Canal, for which the Salwarpe provides the water supply. At the time of writing the next section of the Barge Canal, through Vines Park, was in the process of re-excavation. Our route continues through Vines Park to the Kidderminster road, which we cross to follow the canal towpath, carefully constructed in a new tunnel that takes the canal through a railway embankment and on under another railway bridge, before emerging, clear and deep, along-

Excavations being carried out by the Herefordshire and Worcestershire County Council Archaeological Department in April 1983, working under pressure before the builders of the new canal arrived at the site. Note the remains of the original wooden stakes (lower foreground); the pilings of the new canal; the trickling of the salt spring (centre right) which fed a brine pit that was worked here during the Middle Ages; and a piece of piping used to carry the brine into a salt works which also once stood here

The newly constructed tunnel through the embankment carrying the Worcester–Birmingham railway at Droitwich

side a factory site. We soon reach the new concrete span of Salwarpe road bridge. The towpath, now reconstructed, was not open when I passed so I had to scramble up the adjacent road embankment and down the other side to gain access to the towpath walk where the canal enters the vast recreation area which now covers the flat valley floor.

The canal soon swings in a slow curve to the left, following the valley edge. The pathway is wide and well maintained, and provides a route to the town for the people who live in the estates beyond. Ahead, a modern wooden-arched footbridge spans the canal and links to a main pathway that crosses the valley floor. Beyond this bridge the towpath closely follows the canal bank, and is segregated from a tarmac path along the edge of the playing fields which offers an easier route. Another tarmaced path follows the left bank of the canal for the next quarter of a mile, through to Siding Lane bridge. The canal along this reach is cut out from the valley side, with a slight embankment providing the towpath walk. By the neat brick bridge is a level area which marks the site of an old wharf that once served Briar Mill, on the Salwarpe, just to the west. Beyond the bridge the former wharf building is now painted and provides a home for the Royal Air Force Association Club headquarters.

The canal is soon crossed by another wooden pedestrian bridge that links the housing estate to the flat fields beyond. May trees and gorse bushes line the right edge of the towpath along this reach. On the far side of the valley is a huge road interchange, which filters traffic on the ring road that bypasses the town. The canal is then traversed by a new concrete bridge. The wide track of the towpath under the bridge is used by the local schoolboys as a hide where they while away their lunch hour, throwing stones into the canal.

Beyond Ombersley Way bridge, the towpath becomes a wide but muddy track and the canal is covered with duckweed. On the left bank a compact new housing estate stands high on the valley side, the lowest house some 15 feet above the canal. The canal soon bends sharply to realign itself to go under a major concrete span of Roman Way, the A38 diversion route, which circles the town. Beyond the bridge, the canal moves out into the countryside.

The River Salwarpe meanders down the valley to the right as the canal curves around to follow the contour of the valley side. Bushes soon give way to open fields on the left bank. Ahead, the tower of Salwarpe church and the chimneys of Salwarpe Court can just be seen.

We soon reach a swing bridge. From this point the next section of the canal is very shallow, and the path itself narrower on entering the deep cutting by Salwarpe church. The canal curves sharply to the left after entering this wooded cutting, and at the far end a high brick bridge spans the canal. The towpath through the cutting is very slippery and needs to be tackled with care. However, a higher-level path follows the top of the cutting on the right, and leads to Salwarpe church.

It is not easy to rejoin the towpath at the far end of Salwarpe cutting, so one has to retrace one's steps to rejoin the cutting at the Droitwich end. Our walk continues along the right bank of the canal. Once under the Salwarpe Bridge, the canal turns very sharply. The towpath edge is lined with sandstone blocks along the tricky reach. Soon after this the canal leaves its cutting and passes over an embankment to cross the valley of a small stream. Down to the right the new Hill End culvert, recently rebuilt by the Trust, is clearly visible, together with a new spill weir. The River Salwarpe itself lies far below on the valley floor. Beyond the embankment the canal enters another short cutting, at the end of which it swings sharply left past another swing bridge.

The canal now takes a high-contour course along the Salwarpe valley side for the next quarter of a mile, and offers exceptional views across the valley. Suddenly the canal turns southwards into another deep cutting, to move away from the Salwarpe valley altogether for a while. The towpath follows the right bank and takes a line some 10 feet above the canal level along the side of this cutting. The canal slowly curves through the cutting and, after a while, the lock at Ladywood comes into view, marking the end of the long summit level of the canal. Within the next mile, a further four locks lower the canal to rejoin the Salwarpe valley. Beyond a concrete bridge the towpath continues along the right bank of the canal to the next lock, where another footpath links to it.

Below the lock, the canal joins the shallow valley carved by Martin's Brook, which is carried in a culvert under the canal just before the next lock is reached. Below this lock, Martin's Brook follows the towpath on the right and is hidden in a mass of undergrowth. A little further down, Lock No. 4 is being rebuilt. The bottom of this lock chamber was water-filled, as was the reed-edged reach below, which gently curved to the left as the canal re-entered the Salwarpe valley. A lane soon joins the right bank, just after a large storage area, and replaces the towpath along the next reach to Porter's Mill.

At Porter's Mill Lock our route follows the adjacent lane to the crossroads beyond. Our signposted path continues southwards from here, along the right bank of the canal. The next reach is quite the most picturesque of all, as the canal sweeps in a huge semicircle around the wooded edge of the Salwarpe valley. A wooded lane follows the left bank for a while before leading southwards – after this the canal offers idyllic peace.

Soon the river and towpath part company as the canal curves to take a westerly course. Ahead, a white-walled mill house and brick outbuildings fill the centre of the valley floor. After crossing a stile, our route along the towpath becomes a little overgrown. The valley narrows to the right. Ahead, through the undergrowth, a brick bridge can be seen crossing the canal. Just before it is Mildenham Lock, with a decrepit lower gate swaying in the wind. A stile takes the towpath on to the drive, which leads to the mill house.

A gap through the hedge on the west side of the drive provides access to the footpath beyond. This time the reed-filled canal is hardly visible at first, but after a while the towpath becomes clearer and beyond a hillock to the right the Salwarpe moves closer to the canal side. A stile bars the towpath and beyond are large water meadows. The canal soon turns sharply to the left, leaving the Salwarpe which crosses to the far side of its flood plain, and then follows a contour path around the edge of the valley floor. The towpath here is of thick springy grass, and makes a pleasant walk as it edges along its own embankment, with bushes dotted about in the meadows beyond.

The canal now heads for the steeply wooded valley side ahead. Just before the canal reaches the steep bank, bushes crowd around the canal sides. Here, hidden underneath them, is a well-preserved brick bridge, with sandstone blocks embedded in the wall still showing deep rope grooves. Ivy grows over the far side of the bridge, camouflaging it. Beyond the bridge the canal turns sharply right and the towpath follows a cleared path through the trees, and after some distance the Salwarpe swings over to butt against the towpath side. The Droitwich Canals Trust have proposed a scheme to link the canal to the river at this point, as one way to overcome an obstruction that lies ahead.

Our path continues in a straight course, with the canal at the foot of the steeply wooded valley side. Suddenly the canal is blocked by a brick barrier – beyond it, a huge earth embankment dams the line. We have a choice of two routes – straight up the slope, or a shallower climb to the right; both lead out to the dual carriageway of the A449, which crosses the valley here. We have to cross the road and our route then takes us to the right along to a field gate on the west side of the road, with a clear signpost: 'Public Footpath to the River'. A stile is clearly marked 'Towpath Walk'. Once over the stile, our path continues westwards along the hedgerow on the left. We cross another stile, from which we can see a gap in the towpath hedge. Here a flat bridge leads across to the private grounds of Hawford Lodge School. On closer inspection, this bridge proves to span the seventh lock, the chamber of which is completely overgrown.

The canal now takes a course almost parallel to the River Severn, which lies just across the fields to the west. Soon the canal line emerges from the scrub and into the garden of a large white house, which stands up on the bank beyond, with a group of older cottages a little to the right. The former junction lock now acts as an ornamental pool, with a bridge spanning it. Beyond, the link to the Severn is tree-lined and overgrown. The River Severn is wide and also tree-lined here. Below the canal junction it takes a sharp swing to the west, with the deep, fast-flowing water eroding the steep river bank. This area provides an idyllic setting to end our walk. The only improvement one could hope for would be to see craft again proceeding up the restored canal, towards Droitwich.

Further reading

C. Hadfield, *Canals of the West Midlands*. David and Charles, 1969.

The Droitwich Canals Trust Booklet.

5

North-west and North-east

The Trent and Mersey Canal

from Middlewich Wharf (SJ 705663) via Stud Green, Wheelock, Hassall Green, Rode Heath and Church Lawton, to the Harecastle Tunnel, Kidsgrove (SJ 837542)
Map 118

PRECEDING PAGE *The Bridgewater Canal under the Hawthorn Lane Aqueduct at Stretford*

The Bridgewater and Trent and Mersey Canals, which were immediately interlinked, perhaps did more than any others to provoke the rush of canal building in England in the 1780s. They owed much to the skill of one man, James Brindley. The prime mover behind the latter scheme was the pottery owner, Josiah Wedgwood. He and his friends Thomas Bentley and Erasmus Darwin helped to marshal parliamentary support for an Act in 1766, which authorized the construction of a navigation from the Trent to Runcorn. The scheme included a tunnel through Harecastle Hill nearly 1¾ miles long, and resulted in a waterway 67 miles long, including fifty-nine locks, when it was opened with much acclaim in 1777. The canal was a great success and one of those who benefited most was Wedgwood, as the vast tonnages of china clay and flint reached his expanded works at Etruria near Stoke-on-Trent, at a substantially reduced transport cost.

The canal's traffic increased to such an extent that by the 1820s the low, narrow Harecastle Tunnel was creating a bottleneck. Thomas Telford was asked to solve the problem and as a result a second tunnel, complete with towpath, was opened in 1827. Its construction took three years against the eleven of the first tunnel, and provided a measure of the extent to which engineering techniques had improved over the intervening fifty years. In the 1830s many of the locks lifting the canal from the Cheshire Plain at Wheelock through to Kidsgrove were duplicated to counteract growing railway competition.

The Trent and Mersey Canal was seen by Brindley as part of a 'Grand Cross', with the Trent and Mersey, like the 'Grand Trunk Canal', having branches to the Severn and Thames. It was not until 1790 that the last major link was achieved with the opening of the Oxford Canal. Even so, long before then, the Staffordshire and Worcestershire Canal had made a connection with the River Severn, while other connections to the Birmingham Canal

Navigations and the Coventry Canal had tapped the valuable coalfields near those towns. These routes brought more trade to the original Brindley line. In consequence the Trent and Mersey Canal was connected with no fewer than eight other canals or significant branches. Perhaps the most spectacular of these links was opened at Anderton in 1875, when a hydraulic-powered lift, designed by E. Leader Williams, allowed craft to be raised or lowered over the 50-foot height difference between the canal and the River Weaver below. This had an immediate impact on the traffic levels along the canal to Middlewich and beyond. Schemes for a Birmingham and Liverpool Ship Canal were discussed but nothing materialized, except that the Trent and Mersey Canal was dredged between Runcorn and the Potteries, and the section between Middlewich and Anderton was enlarged in 1891 to carry wide barges.

The Trent and Mersey Canal was never without costly maintenance problems. Many arose from the actual industries which it served: the greatest expense was incurred in the mid-Cheshire area where vast salt mines extended under the canal. As these mines became worked out, so the ground above subsided, causing the flashes now so prevalent there; these were especially marked in the area around Thurlwood and Rode Heath. Subsidence was so rapid that at one stage the River Wheelock diverted its course and flooded local mines, with the result that salt extraction had to be abandoned. Even so, the subsidence continued unabated, and at Thurlwood in particular it seriously damaged both the lock and overbridge, and they had to be replaced. Elsewhere, embankments had to be constantly raised and other structures reinforced. However, what is more important to us is the fact that the canal has survived intact, even though all its commercial traffic has long since ceased.

Our exploration takes us along one of the most interesting sections of the canal and provides the chance to see how well this once leading industrial transport artery has now adapted to its new role as a 'Cruiseway'. There is no better place to start than Middlewich Wharf, just south of a bridge that carries the A54 Congleton road over the canal.

Middlewich is historically a salt town, but the industry has long since moved from the central area. Fortunately, however, the old wharf and its warehouse, together with land further on beside the locks, are now considered a conservation area to which access from the main road is readily gained through a wide gateway on the left, opposite St Michael's church.

The well-used towpath follows the right bank and quickly leads to two single locks, both in a sad state of repair. Above the second lock the canal makes a 90 degree turn to the right. On the opposite bank is an interesting example of an old dry dock. Above the next lock we reach one of the many old canal yards that now have been converted to hire boat bases.

Beyond the yard a brick bridge, marked with a plate stating 'No. 169', provides a frame for a view of the adjacent canal junction. Here a symmetrical arch lifts the towpath over the entrance to the Wardle Canal; a keystone on that bridge bears the date 1829. The junction creates a tight blind turn.

The neat King's Lock public house stands on the left bank immediately above the junction area, and has a well-used beer garden that extends to the lockside wall. Just before the lock, on the west bank, the A533 road joins the canal side and closely parallels it for the next 2 miles. The towpath follows a causeway between the two, although for a while the height of the canal offers some protection from the noisy road.

The canal is soon crossed by the ornate concrete Cledford Bridge, which provides access to the modern British Salt factory that lies beyond. A little further on a second factory dwarfs the compact red-brick lock house and the black metal split bridge before the lock. Beyond this lock, the canal passes close by the vast RHM Foods factory and a main road crosses the canal. Two lone locks follow each other and are almost overwhelmed by the parallel road. They lift the canal up into the countryside, which soon attracts the waterway to move away to the east of Elworth and Sandbach.

At Stud Green, a brick bridge takes Dragon Lane over the canal. Beyond the bridge the grassy towpath, protected by a hedge, offers an ideal country walk. On the right bank an old sawmill still has the fast-flowing lock by-wash running underneath. Ahead, the narrow lock is in prime condition, resplendent with new gates. A small basin area above the lock offers a mooring for passing boats, and beyond it a new metal span bridge crosses the canal.

The problem of subsidence caused by the old salt workings is especially evident over the next couple of miles. The whole area to the west of the canal is a mixture of abandoned salt workings,

One of the canal's distinctive cast-iron mileposts. Replicas are being produced by the Trent and Mersey Canal Society to replace those lost; this is an original

and fields inundated with water because the drainage of the area has been upset. The canal winds along a contour for this reach and has been carefully banked with concrete and steel piles. For quite a distance a trackway follows the towpath line to allow speedy access for machinery should the need arise. In other places back-filling has made the towpath uneven, but the bank more secure.

On the left bank a huge factory, untidily clad with asbestos sheeting, makes a noisy background to the canal. A little later, on the right, an old cottage tilts markedly, undermined by the salt workings below. The scene here is austere, with a strange mixture of farms and the hotch-potch of the outskirts of a town.

Ahead, the embankment of a railway line strides across the lower-lying land to the right, with a large flash covering the valley floor. For a while along this reach, the towpath side seems to be composed of coal dust. On the right a little row of cottages connects to a canal wharf that has long since closed. Ahead, the canal and the railway spar before it finally finds a path under the line. Just before this bridge a railway and canal interchange area on the left bank lies derelict and in decay.

Once beyond the railway embankment, the canal moves out into more pleasant countryside, following a contour path around the fields. The towpath hedgerow here is dotted with larger trees. A culvert soon takes a small brook in a leafy cutting, under the canal. Beyond, a brick bridge enables a farm track to cross the line. The canal creeps around another curve, and after the towpath passes under a new concrete bridge the scenery briefly improves.

Once beyond the quarry plant on the left bank, the canal turns east. Beyond lies the village of Wheelock, which seems to straddle the canal. At first a storage building and some cottages line the towpath edge. The canal slides under a stout brick-arched bridge to reach the grassy wharf area; the old warehouse here is used as a motor repair works, while the wharf itself is overlooked by a white cottage.

Once the canal leaves Wheelock it begins its steep climb from the Cheshire plain. A flight of eight locks, all until recently paired, lift the canal 80 feet in just over a mile. First the canal passes over a small brick aqueduct across a local stream. Ahead lies a wide double bridge which precedes the first locks of the flight; the twin span was not the original structure, and it is easy to identify the old and the new sections. Beside the lock the original lock houses are still preserved. Another pair of locks quickly follows before the canal edges past the abutments of an old railway bridge.

Another pair of locks lies a little way ahead, and beyond them the canalside settlement of Malkins Bank is visible. The canal divides to go under another set of twin-arched bridges and the towpath emerges by a pair of locks, placed between two long rows of cottages that line the canal side.

Just above the village, a canal arm leaves to the right under a bridge. The dockside here is now grassed over and the water provides another bunker for the golf course that extends beyond. The right-hand chamber of the next pair of locks has been weired, and now provides an alcove to store a canal maintenance boat. Ahead are two more pairs of locks, preceded by their distinctive guarding bridges. The canal is now out in the open countryside, though the horizon is soon dominated by an embankment that takes the M6 motorway across the fields.

Once under the motorway, some semblance of calm returns. Ahead lies another pair of lone locks amidst the fields. A painted sign warns boaters that the lock to the right only offers a beam of 6 feet 10 inches and must not be used by wider craft! Beyond these locks the sleepy hamlet of Hassall Green comes into view. Ahead, a concrete bridge crosses the canal and hides the single lock.

Once the canal leaves Hassall Green, it takes up a winding course through the fields before resuming a contour line. After a while, the first of the two single Pierpoint Locks come into view. Between the locks is a bridge. After the Pierpoint Locks the canal is at its prettiest. In the far distance the heights of Harecastle Hill can just be seen. A hawthorn hedge lines the towpath bank and creates a private pathway through the fields beyond. Soon the canal reaches the steep edge of a tree-lined valley and takes up a firm contour line. The towpath goes under another elegant farm bridge; beyond, a narrow but deep valley, with a road at its foot, is spanned by a brick aqueduct.

After a time market gardens and nurseries begin to dominate the fields on either side of the canal. The canal passes into a shallow cutting before reaching another paired arched bridge, beyond which lies the Lower Thurlwood set of locks, and beside them a well-maintained lock cottage.

This must be one of the most frequently glimpsed canal bridges in the country. It lies a few hundred yards to the west of the M6 crossover

A bumpy track parallels the canal on the approach to the Thurlwood Steel Lock. To the left the straggling village of Rode Heath can be seen, a bridge providing a vantage point to survey the strange structure that lies ahead, replacing the right of the two original lock chambers. The Steel Lock was conceived in 1957 as the ideal way to combat the subsidence prevalent at this point. The theory was that the whole lock chamber could be bodily jacked up if it sank into the ground. In practice it proved so difficult to use and maintain that it is now simply a monument to an idea that failed. All boats currently use the conventional lock which stands by its side.

The section above the lock is quite a pleasant reach. Just before the next bridge, the compact Broughton Arms backs on to the canal. Canalside benches and flowering trees make it an attractive spot for the locals and visitors alike.

Just after the bridge lies a timber yard, partly hidden behind some bushes, and the smell of sawdust drifts across the canal. Beyond the towpath edge the valley drops steeply away to the right, as the canal follows a contour path. After a while the canal bends sharply to go under the A50 road. Beyond, the canal passes over a small lane on a high brick-built aqueduct.

Another flight of locks – six, all paired – come in quick succession, lifting the canal some 57 feet through a pleasant, thinly wooded area. Ahead, the peak of Mow Cop stands out on the skyline through the haze. Halfway up the flight, at bridge No. 137, the towpath transfers to the left-hand bank. Once beyond the remaining three locks, the canal circles round in a shallow cutting, with a group of beach trees on the towpath side.

The canal soon passes a farm on the right and then curves sharply to the left to rise up the Red Bull flight of locks, the first three of which are visible to the south like a grassy staircase in front of a row of tall trees, as they climb up through the fields.

By the time the second pair of locks is reached the water has taken on a rusty hue, and along the pound above the third lock even the banks at the water's edge have a thick orange film. Ahead are the white wharf buildings of the British Waterways Red Bull yard with, beyond, a new concrete span over the canal. The railed towpath threads its way underneath to reach a single lock with the Red Bull public house by the right-hand bank.

Above the lock, on the right, a variety of boats are moored. High above them some old wharf buildings are now used as a boat yard and canal ware shop. Ahead, the solid brick arch of the Telford-designed Macclesfield Canal aqueduct crosses the canal. Beyond it, another pair of locks lifts the canal ever upward towards the hills ahead. A little further on, the towpath lifts over an old canal arm and soon reaches a dirty grey steel bridge beyond which lies another pair of locks; beside the bridge is the Canal Tavern.

On the lock island between these locks, an old toll office remains unused; beyond, the metal span of the main London to Manchester railway line looms. The towpath transfers to the right at the locks and, just before reaching the railway bridge, a neat stone bridge lifts it over the entrance to the Macclesfield Canal, which joins from the right.

After passing under the railway, the canal turns sharply to the right and soon enters a cutting to pass under a blue-brick bridge which takes a road to Kidsgrove Station forecourt. As we get closer to the mouth of Harecastle Tunnel, the water becomes a deeper orange, coloured by the ironstone under Harecastle Hill.

Ahead, another low multi-arched span carries trains over the canal line. Beyond, a brick bridge takes the towpath across to the tunnel mouth. However, the towpath through the tunnel was removed many years ago.

Our walk along the Trent and Mersey Canal ends here. By walking a short distance back along the towpath, just under the first railway bridge, a fenced pathway provides access to Kidsgrove Station car park. Buses back to Rode Heath, Malkins Bank, Sandbach and Middlewich stop in Liverpool Road, at the other end of the station approach.

Further reading

Peter Lead, *The Trent and Mersey Canal: Historic Waterways Scenes*. Moorland Publishing, 1980.

Jean Lindsay, *The Trent and Mersey Canal*. David and Charles, 1979.

The Bridgewater Canal

from Dean Road, Sale (SJ 795932) via Stretford, Trafford Park, Barton upon Irwell, Patricroft, Monton and Worsley village to the Delph (SD 738005)
Map 109

In 1752 James Brindley was employed to drain Wet Earth colliery, Clifton, on the banks of the Irwell. His knowledge of hydraulics enabled him to solve that problem by the use of an ingenious water-powered pump. It was partly because of this that the Duke of Bridgewater and his agent, John Gilbert, employed Brindley to assist them in the development of the scheme to drain the Duke's mines at Worsley and get the coal cheaply transported into Manchester. It was not until after July 1759 that Brindley entered the development of the scheme which the Duke and John Gilbert had presented in detail to the House of Commons, seeking approval for their plans for the canal to Salford and a branch to Hollins Ferry. The first scheme went wrong and a second was developed for which a new Act was sought. Brindley's evidence to Parliament was crucial in two respects. First, he had to convince members that the Duke's new scheme would not take water away from the Mersey and Irwell Navigation, which had opened in 1734, and second, he had to convince them that an aqueduct high over the Irwell was both feasible and practicable. He demonstrated these ideas by making a model of the aqueduct out of cheese. He won support for the second Act, and as a result was given the job of engineer in charge of building the aqueduct. Here he introduced for the first time the idea of 'clay puddling' to make the walls impervious to water. It is interesting to recall that this original aqueduct nearly collapsed when first built by Brindley, but later was so well strengthened by John Gilbert that afterwards it became almost indestructible.

Brindley was a hydraulics engineer of repute. He had extensive experience of the use of fall, and of the employment and complexities of water. He was a practical realist, in that he never over-extended his art, and believed that by following contours where possible and avoiding cuttings, embankments and other costly technicalities he would achieve the most reliable canal. Above all else, Brindley was a fervent believer in canals and used publicity to great advantage. It was Brindley, more than anyone else, who subsequently spread the idea of arterial canals throughout England – he was personally involved in bringing twenty-two schemes to fruition.

By 1757 profit levels from the Duke of Bridgewater's mines at Worsley were flagging because the pits were beginning to fill with water. The Duke appointed one of his land agents, John Gilbert, to resolve the difficulties. Gilbert solved the problem by suggesting that if a tunnel into the mines was large enough to carry barges they could move the coal to the market. The water in the mines would provide the supply for the canal for the barges to travel along, and as a result the flooded coalmines could be drained. It was a simple idea, yet it worked! In 1761 the canal was opened to Stretford and coal prices were halved. By 1765, the line reached Castlefield Wharf in Manchester, with the same effect.

The Duke of Bridgewater gained a third Act in 1762 to enable him to extend the canal from Stretford through to the tideway at Runcorn. Disputes with landowners at the Runcorn end delayed the work, and it was not until March 1776 that this extension was opened. Well before then, the profitability of the Worsley to Castlefield section was being proved. Equally, the Mersey and Irwell Navigation was also benefiting from extra trade as it carried coal through to Salford Quay, being supplied by gig crane hoist, which transferred the cargoes from craft on the Barton Aqueduct into Mersey Flats below.

In the nineteenth century the canal developed a triple trade, transporting raw cotton to the mills, providing the furnaces of the mills with coal, and then taking the finished products away. In 1845 the Bridgewater Estate Trustees purchased their old rival, the Mersey and Irwell Navigation, and in 1872 the Bridgewater Navigation Company was formed. The canal was purchased by the Manchester Ship Canal Company, under the rights granted by their Act, so that they could replace the original Brindley aqueduct with a swing aqueduct which could carry the older canal across the new Ship Canal. This was opened in 1893, and the original Brindley aqueduct removed.

The canal trade continued to flourish until the 1950s when the cotton trade finally died. Mine closures in the 1960s ultimately removed the coal traffic that had led to the construction of the canal some two hundred years before. By that time pleasure craft were beginning to use the canal, and these, together with trip boats, have now provided it with a new lease of life.

Our exploration covers part of the old main line, now called the Leigh branch, from Worsley to Stretford, together with a short section of the Runcorn line, which was linked to the Trent and Mersey Canal at Preston Brook. The walk starts at Dane Road bridge, Sale, adjacent to the railway station, which is on the south side of the Runcorn line. Access to the towpath on the north bank can be gained either through the Bridge Inn car park on the left, or along a private slip road which runs along the north of Dane Road. Either route takes us northwards along the canal bank, quickly leaving the suburbs of Sale behind.

For the first mile or so, the canal banks are lined with sandstone blocks, impressive for both their size and strength. We pass the Manchester University Boat Club on our left and soon the lane, the canal and the railway are crossed by a massive concrete span; the huge supporting pillars separating the towpath from the lane and the railway from the canal.

After a short distance the canal goes over an aqueduct which crosses the narrow River Mersey. Beyond the aqueduct the towpath becomes a wide and muddy track, open and well used by cyclists and walkers going to and from work. On both banks of the River Mersey a flood plain ensures a wide corridor of open land, with fields for horses and some crops. For the next quarter of a mile the right bank is lined with a continuous string of moored boats.

We soon pass over another small aqueduct, with the narrow Bourne Lane passing underneath. This announces the start of suburbia, and the outskirts of Stretford. Passing under Edge Lane bridge, Stretford, a separate metal span conveys a footpath over the canal. Horse steps are set into the towpath edge, just before this bridge, on the right of which is Stretford Station.

Beyond Edge Lane bridge the towpath is paralleled by a red-brick wall, which protects the houses beyond from the vandals who regularly spray slogans on it. Over the rooftops and to the left the church tower is quite close. In between, beyond the towpath wall, a row of cottages is being restored. Ahead a dilapidated shed spans a dry dock: this is Rathbone Brothers' Longford Dry Dock. Beyond it, the canal curves northwards and soon passes beneath a large gaspipe which spans the canal just before the new Longford Road bridge.

The canal stretches out ahead like a long, wide, silver road. At first industry lines either bank, but the towpath is wide and clear. Ahead, a series of bridges and pipes cross the canal. A span of a former railway branch can be seen beyond the furthest bridge. Here we reach the junction of the 'old' and 'new' lines: the spot is aptly named Waters Meeting. The whole area seems ideal for fish and many local fishermen congregate along the banks. The canal to the right leads to Castlefield Junction, while the branch ahead is the original course that linked the mines at Worsley to Stretford in 1761. At one stage a bridge took the Castlefield towpath across the canal at this point; now only the bridge supports remain. Walkers wishing to go to Manchester have to walk a short way along the 'old' line to Taylors Bridge, and then retrace their steps along the opposite bank. It is interesting to consider that there are 28 lock-free miles of canal between Manchester and Runcorn, and a further 11 miles along the Leigh branch; those long levels, no doubt, owe much to Brindley's keen eye.

Beyond Taylors Bridge the canal was built wide enough to allow two Mersey flats to pass. Now the canal bends slowly to the right, choosing a wide path between the factories that line its banks. Soon another straight reach of canal lies ahead, bridged by various pipes between the industrial complexes on either bank; chemical factories and engineering works both vie for space in the extensive Trafford Park Industrial Estate. All provide a constant barrage of noise alongside the canal. In places, the large stone slabs which lined the canal banks have been removed and new metal piling inserted in their place.

The towpath crosses a small side arm, now used as a cooling pond for the works beyond: steam jets spray across the water. We soon pass under a main road bridge, after which the canal banks are lined with more works – on the right is the large ICI plant, and on the left huge grain silos. The towpath with its grassy edges pushes a green way through this otherwise industrialized landscape, hiding behind high concrete planked walls.

Ahead, an array of factory chimneys dominates the horizon. Soon a high, new, single-span concrete road bridge crosses the canal, carrying a dual carriageway from the industrial estate to link with the motorway. The earth embankment dominates the flat surrounding plain. Beyond this bridge a line of tall poplar trees graces the canal bank, shielding it from the huge engineering works on the right. The canal stretches out ahead, a wide expanse

DEATH
TO SCOUSERS
HELMET

Under the railway viaduct by Waters Meeting. The man is carrying an air rifle, which he was using to shoot at bottles floating in the canal

of water, now little used by boats, crossing the flat landscape of the former marshland known as Trafford Moss.

After passing a tall water tower on the left, and a bridge carrying cable ducts over the canal, with beyond it a green-painted metal road bridge, we reach an old railway bridge, rusted and decayed. Soon the towpath rises over a filled-in arm. Ahead the canal curves round to cross the Barton Aqueduct, a row of worn wooden mooring bollards lining the towpath edge. Turning the bend, the imposing entrance of the aqueduct itself comes into view; this structure turns to allow larger craft to pass along the Manchester Ship Canal, which the Bridgewater Canal crosses at this point.

When we reach the edge of the Ship Canal there is no towpath across the aqueduct, and we have to make a detour along a pathway to the left which leads out to Barton Road bridge, another swing bridge over the Ship Canal, from which we can get a perfect view of the aqueduct. The 234-foot-long steel tank, surrounded with its own girder bridge, pivots on an island in the centre of the Ship Canal. The water in the tank is 6 feet deep and 18 feet wide. To make way for Ship Canal traffic, the whole 1,500-ton structure is able to turn some 90 degrees while still full of water. It is a unique and impressive sight, making a worthy successor to the original Brindley Aqueduct which it replaced.

It is possible to go down to the Ship Canal towpath to inspect the end of the old aqueduct and see the water seal of the new line. A set of white railed steps proceeds down the embankment at the bridge end. There is no way through, so we must retrace our steps to continue along Barton Bridge Road to the crossroads beyond, where to the right Barton Lane passes under a yellow-painted aqueduct. In Barton Lane, a tablet on the left side recounts that the stone arch of the Brindley Aqueduct near this point was moved to allow Barton Lane to be widened in 1898. The mason's marks are visible on the stone blocks.

We continue northwards over the crossroads, following the left bank of the canal and passing the Bridgewater Canal Company Engineers Yard and Wharf on the right. Soon afterwards we regain the towpath, which continues to be paralleled by the busy road. On the right we pass a former wharf area and a canal arm, both of which lie derelict.

After a while we reach a busy road bridge which takes the A35 Warrington to Salford road over the canal. Beside the bridge is an

Masons' marks on the stonework of the Brindley Aqueduct

ornate brick building and before the bridge, on the right, another small arm has been filled in to provide a coach park. The canal now curves slowly to the right and passes under a pedestrian bridge and a busy railway bridge. Ahead, a large factory chimney dominates the skyline; the canal wharf here is no longer used. Soon we pass under the grey span of another road bridge. Walking towards Monton, we pass under the wide concrete span of a new motorway link road. The canal now bends sharply to the left, heading towards Worsley; after the bend, the canal passes under another girder road bridge.

From Monton Bridge the canal takes on a tree-lined air as it moves on to a low embankment. No doubt the lowering of the surrounding land has been partly caused by the extensive mining works. A row of small gardens reaches up to the foot of the embankment on the left; on the right are woods, a golf course and fields. The canal stretches out in a long, straight line ahead, between its newly embanked edges. In the midst of the embankment, the canal widens to create a turning point. Ahead, over the trees, we can see the spire of Worsley church, and as we get closer to Worsley the canal water becomes a rusty colour, caused by iron-stained water leaving the old mine workings. On the right, larger houses line the canal bank, with woods beyond. We now come to a disused wharf. The canal narrows beyond it, the water now a deep orange. On the right we pass the Cheshire

The Delph: an entrance to the Duke's unique underground canal system. Might there be some potential here for a new addition to our existing industrial museums?

Plain Hire Cruisers base. Worsley Dry Docks have a site next door, with covered sheds and a black and white façade; this is now a modern working boatyard servicing hire craft.

The towpath leads out to a pleasant green where an ornate metal pedestrian bridge crosses the canal to link with a larger, tree-lined village green beyond. The green backdrop on either side heightens the contrast. The towpath follows the left bank as it curves left past the Packet House, while the arm to the Delph leads off to the right. We soon pass under a road bridge which spans the cutting. A slope links to the towpath here and enables us to circle back to the road and cross the canal. On the right, a path leads down to the Packet House and on to the mine entrance.

The view of the canal from the Packet House steps is unique: it was from these steps that packet boats conveyed their passengers in great comfort to Castlefield, a service which lasted until 1872. The path takes us past the Packet House and across an overbridge, which crosses the entrance to the Delph. The actual mine entrances can be studied more closely by following the path forward to the road beyond, where we cross by the offices of Miller, Metcalfe and Co., estate agents, and turn left to the Delph viewing point, which provides a lasting memorial to the mines. A single starvationer – the working boats so-called because of their projecting ribs – lies in the rust-coloured water below, with the old sluice mechanisms beyond. A notice reminds visitors that there were 46 miles of underground canals to the north of the Delph; these lay on two main levels, connected with a water-powered incline plane – an engineering masterpiece in its own right. These mines brought the Duke of Bridgewater his fortune and the people of Manchester cheap coal. The Worsley Mine entrance is the ideal end for our walk – it is the place where it all started.

Further reading

H. Malet, *The Canal Duke*. David and Charles, 1961.

H. Malet, *Coal, Cotton and Canals*. Neil Richardson, 1981.

H. Malet, *Bridgewater, The Canal Duke 1736–1803*. Manchester University Press, 1977.

G. Wheat, *On the Duke's Cut*. Transport Publishing, 1977.

The Huddersfield Narrow Canal

from Mottram Road, Stalybridge (SJ 966987) via Mossley, Greenfield and Uppermill to Diggle Tunnel mouth, then from Marsden Tunnel mouth to Slaithwaite (SE 079140)
Maps 109 and 110

There is seemingly nothing that evokes more interest than a trans-Pennine canal. However, the fascination of all the transport routes over the Pennines, whether they be packhorse, turnpike or railway, cannot be matched by the extraordinary Standedge Tunnel, the highest and longest canal tunnel in Britain.

The Huddersfield Narrow Canal was the third and shortest of all the trans-Pennine waterway routes – a mere 20 miles – but it was certainly not a modest canal. It had the highest summit level at 648 feet, while the 3-mile 418-yards-long Standedge Tunnel, carved through rock, was a masterpiece in its own right. The canal was conceived as a link between the two heartlands of the mill industry, served by the Ashton and Huddersfield Broad Canals. Work started in 1794 under the direction of Benjamin Outram, who was asked to complete the sections between Ashton and Stalybridge and Huddersfield and Slaithwaite with all speed, to capture trade. By 1798 the Canal was open from Ashton to Wool Road, to the west of the Pennines, and between Huddersfield and Marsden on the east. Transfer wharfs were built at these points, and a packhorse route established to link the two. The construction of Standedge Tunnel proved harder and more expensive than originally anticipated, and it nearly bankrupted the canal company. Work was finally completed in December 1810, and on 4 April 1811 the canal was opened throughout, some fifteen years after the original plans were laid and some six years after its rival, the broad-gauge Rochdale Canal. The cost had been enormous, as the canal had seventy-four narrow locks, while the demands of local millowners for preservation of their water rights necessitated the construction of ten reservoirs.

The canal never proved a commercial success, unlike its great neighbour and rival the Rochdale Canal, and it took thirteen years before the shareholders received their first dividend. Problems occurred with the tunnel, while the narrow locks, which could not accommodate the boats off the broad-gauge navigations of the north-east, meant that most of its traffic tended to be short-haul at either end. In consequence the canal company found later railway competition too great and sold out to the Huddersfield and Manchester Railway in 1844. Three years later the railway had built its own tunnel through Standedge, and the demise of the canal's trade became inevitable. Regular traffic over the summit level ceased in about 1905, by which time maintenance cost was far exceeding receipts, but short-haul runs on the lower reaches continued until World War II. Apart from a short section in Huddersfield, the canal was abandoned in 1944; the remaining length followed in 1963, since which time about 10 per cent of the channel has been filled in.

The last recorded through voyage took place in 1948, when Tom Rolt and Robert Aickman managed to take the boat *Ailsa Craig* between Ashton and Huddersfield. Subsequently the lock gates were removed, and the locks either capped or filled. Fortunately the channel remained as a water supply to local industry, and recently the pressures of the Huddersfield Canal Society have begun to bear fruit both in protecting the canal, opening the towpath as a leisure route, and in restoring the waterway. For the time being it is for the most part unnavigable, so the walker has the unique opportunity to explore it throughout.

Our walk is in two parts, and covers both the western and eastern approaches to Standedge Tunnel. For the very energetic they can be linked by following the route of Boat Lane over the top. Our exploration starts at Mottram Road, Stalybridge, where a road-widening scheme has obliterated the canal. To the south of the road a new warehouse has been built across the canal line. Our route takes us forward to the Mottram Road Basin area, just to the north of a filled in, culverted lock chamber. The base of an old crane identifies the decay. The water in the canal is clear but full of rubbish. At first the towpath, muddy in places, creeps along the backs of garages to the right of the canal. Here some young trees have been planted on the canalside bank to improve the view. Our path then passes under a disused railway bridge, beyond which it runs along the right-hand side of the valley floor after passing under a stone bridge. Allotments segregate the canal from a high and disused railway embankment on the right. Along the valley floor a variety of houses and factories create a jumbled view. Ahead, the towers of Hartshead power station dominate the landscape. The towpath has a firm stone edge and soon becomes quite rural, with horses grazing in a rough pasture to the right. The River Tame parallels the canal on the left.

After a while we reach the perimeter of the power station grounds, where the canal, for no apparent reason, has been culverted for about 400 yards. The canal line is now grassed over, but the pathway still remains, passing between the legs of a huge pylon which has been built on the valley floor. Because the filling in of the canal has disrupted drainage, the path is in places a little waterlogged. After a while the extinct canal emerges again, above a hump in the ground which marks the place of another filled-in lock. A few paces further on, just by the power station, the site of a former swing bridge has been culverted to facilitate traffic flows. The wharf above now lies weed-filled and derelict. Our path continues along the right bank of the canal. Although the power station dominates the left bank, the path ahead passes through a leafy glade.

We soon reach a picturesque deep stone lock, which has been filled in to create a dramatic waterfall. We quickly approach a second lock, with a stone bridge crossing the entrance channel. Above the lock the valley becomes more wooded and willows have taken root in the canal line itself.

The canal follows a course cut out high along the valley side, with the fast-flowing river at the foot of a steep bank and some distance below. The towpath is muddy in places, but well used, especially by school groups from the Hartshead Field Study Centre. Small streams tumble down the hillside and cross the towpath; stepping stones have been provided to aid the walker.

Soon rocky valley sides show how tight the river valley has become. Ahead another capped lock lifts the canal line. Looking back, we can see the extent that the canal has risen by simple comparison with the tops of the towers of the power station. Above the next lock, the parallel course of a former railway line enters a tunnel. The canal itself curves to enter the bricked-up mouth of Scout Tunnel, cut through a rocky outcrop to bypass the ravine in which the river flows some 30 feet below. Originally the towpath passed through the tunnel, but now, as it is blocked, our path skirts along the river's edge and climbs up over the rocks, to regain the canal side some 150 yards ahead.

Looking forward from above the northern tunnel mouth, we see the massive Pennine peaks way ahead. This whole area was once a derelict tip and has been converted into a pleasant country park. Above the next lock the remains of an old wharf provide a well-used picnic area in stark contrast to the industrial area beyond. A low-level concrete bridge crosses this lock chamber, and our path uses it to rejoin the towpath on the right-hand bank.

The next section of canal has been dredged. It continues along its valley route, with new warehouse buildings high on the right bank and the spire of All Saints' church, Micklehurst, beyond. The new concrete span of Egmont Street bridge crosses the canal and beyond it we enter an industrial area, with factories on either side and even more rubbish in and along the canal. We then reach another new bridge, carrying Micklehurst Road over the canal. Beyond the bridge the canal snakes round past a large brick mill before we reach another filled-in lock, with a wharf and cottages below. A wide stretch of water continues along the valley, past a dilapidated mill structure and leading to the vast red-brick hulk of Milton Mill, with its ornate tower.

Canal users at Mossley

Just beyond the mill the canal bends sharply to the right to reach another lock and a bridge, which takes the towpath to the left bank. Here is another picnic site. Just above the lock lies an old mill wharf, where disused coal chutes lead into the mill grounds.

The next reach of canal is very weedy indeed, with bulrushes completely filling the canal line in places. The whole valley here has a downtrodden look. Soon a new low-level bridge takes a footpath across the canal. Ahead, in front of a gasholder, is the Tollemache Arms public house, and by it another filled lock, with a picnic site alongside. On the right bank a network of footpaths extends through a landscaped area to new houses on the hillside beyond. To the left, a sturdy stone bridge carries the Manchester road over the River Tame.

The canal continues to wind along the backs of old cottages, and ahead another old bridge has been replaced with a new concrete span. Beyond this a lock is weired, with water cascading down. A footbridge takes the towpath over the tail of the lock to the right bank. The towpath is muddy here, but large blocks along the canal edge make a dry walkway, except where they have tumbled into the canal. We soon reach another lock, the filling in of which has created a pretty waterfall. The towpath passes under an arched bridge which once marked the former county boundary. Beyond and to the right, cricket grounds have a prime position in the centre of the valley floor. Soon the River Tame passes under the sturdy stone-arched Royal George Aqueduct, which carries the canal and towpath across to the left of the valley floor. Beyond this aqueduct a line of trees parallels the towpath embankment on the right. We reach another filled-in lock, after which the towpath passes under another bridge; beyond it another lock is weired. A path leads off to the right, giving access to the Royal George Mills. Beyond the lock the towpath widens and the whole reach above is idyllic.

Our route rises to a road, under which the canal is culverted, which we cross to rejoin the towpath opposite. To the left, the site of the former Manns Wharf now lies derelict and overgrown. The towpath follows a slight embankment on the right. Way ahead a single stone obelisk dominates the horizon on a Pennine peak. After a while, an access bridge crosses the canal, and we pass a local rugby ground.

The canal then reaches the busy A635 Chew valley road, and is culverted under it; our route regains the towpath by crossing this road. The canal is cut out deeply from the valley side along the next reach. We come now to another narrow lock-tail bridge, beyond which Hall's Lock has been filled in. Here the towpath rises alongside the lock, and below the river parallels the towpath side.

Our route soon rises to cross the Oldham road, where we pass a capped lock chamber, to continue along the wooded left bank of the canal. The towpath all along this pretty section has a gravelled surface and provides a popular local walk. In a while we reach a roving bridge, which transfers the towpath to the right bank. A neat row of old stone cottages lines the canal here. The canal follows the curve of the valley edge, and in the valley floor below the River Tame circles around a playing field and passes over a weir, where stepping stones provide access to the towpath.

Ahead lie two restored locks. Beyond, the canal passes over the 'Old Sag' aqueduct, after which a short section of canal leads on the right to the new Brownhill Visitor Centre, where literature about the Tame valley can be obtained. Our path crosses Dobcross New Road and continues forward along the filled-in bed of the canal for a short distance until the open channel is reached at a winding point, where picnic tables are set at the side of the canal. To the right is the restored Wool Road warehouse, which acted as the trans-shipment point at the head of the navigation for the eleven years until Standedge Tunnel was opened. The canal is culverted under Wool Road bridge; we have to cross the road to rejoin the towpath on the other side where a footpath sign points to 'Diggle'. Ahead, a flight of locks stretches out up the valley side, lifting the canal alongside the railway embankment, which parallels the right-hand bank. A turning basin and old wharf area are situated at the bottom of this lock flight.

To the left of the canal the valley floor widens for a while. Ahead a Gothic mill building with a large water tower graces the canalside at the top of the flight of locks. Beside the second lock a '12' milestone is visible at the towpath edge. The remaining locks now come in quick succession until we reach the former Dobcross Loom Works on the left; the view back down the valley from this spot is quite spectacular. Our route crosses to the left of the canal at the lock-tail bridge and continues on across a wharf, past more locks, to go under a disused girder bridge. Ahead housing estates, which make up the settlement at Diggle, are arranged higgledy-piggledy over the valley side.

The canal passes the site of former railway sidings on the right, and we go across Ward Lane where a cottage stands by the far lock side. Between the lock and the lane bridge an unusual metal trough takes a small brook over the canal.

We now pass into a landscaped grassy area – a former wharf – with the dark outline of Warth Mills (1919) ahead. Beyond the wharf the canal climbs through another filled-in lock chamber to reach its summit level, which feels its way in a wide curve to the entrance to Standedge Tunnel. Just before the unusual tunnel mouth, the canal crosses over Diggle Brook on a high aqueduct. The tunnel itself, now firmly gated, looks more like the entrance to an air-raid shelter. A date of 1893 confirms that this was an adaptation of the original line, which was modified when the main line railway alongside was built. Ahead, the heights of the Pennines tower far above. Our path leads up to the road through the Diggle village hall car park, from which we can either return down the valley by bus or continue uphill along Boat Lane, to find the other end of the tunnel, on the east of the Pennine Ridge, at Marsden.

The tunnel end at Marsden can either be approached along the canal towpath from Marsden Station, or, for those who follow the route to Boat Lane, from a short spur called Ainsley Lane, which leaves to the left of the A62. This brings us down beside the now silted tunnel-end reservoir. The whole tunnel mouth area at Marsden is an impressive sight, with the trains emerging from the larger railway tunnel almost above the gated canal tunnel portal. To the left, a staircase weir carries water across over the railway line and down into the canal below. Above all this, the rocky backdrop of the Pennines stands supreme.

An information board near the tunnel mouth cottages explains the scene. A well-kept British Waterways Board maintenance yard lies adjacent to the tunnel end wharf, with an imposing warehouse standing beside the small basin area. Beyond this yard, the canal turns tightly under a girder railway bridge and proceeds in its own cutting along the summit level with the towpath on the right.

The canal snakes along for nearly a mile, with the water clear and deep. Above the valley sides, the high, windswept moors dominate the landscape. To the right, a stream feeds a mill pool in the valley below. Just before the canal reaches Marsden Station, on the left, it passes under a bridge which offers access to a lane.

We soon reach the summit lock by the platform of Marsden Station, where a lockside gate leads out to Station Road and a public house. Beyond the lock, the canal and towpath creep down under two bridges which follow in quick succession, and then sweep round to reach another lock. (These locks are being restored during 1985 as part of a scheme to revive the canal through to Slaithwaite.) Ahead, a tall mill chimney stands imposingly on the skyline. The lines of cold grey houses provide a backdrop to the sloping valley sides as the canal wends its way down towards Huddersfield. To the right, mills and their cottages identify the industry which once brought wealth to the area. Soon we pass another capped lock and a road, and continue on the right bank of the canal, along the backs of some houses, past another lock. The pounds between these locks are wide enough to supply enough water to work the flight. We soon pass another capped lock and reach a cleared section of canal as it passes some well-maintained gardens on the left. The canal's route now moves away from the houses to meet a wooded reach. Down to the right a little stream wends its way along the valley floor; a little further on, a weir diverts water to a mill leat along a contour course.

After a longer rural pound we reach another capped lock, making a strange little tunnel over the canal. To the left steeply sloping fields enclosed by dry stone walls creep down to the canal, making ideal pastures for sheep. The railway now runs high on the valley side above these fields. Soon we reach a large pool alongside the canal; this is Sparth reservoir, which feeds the canal a little further along through a stepped overflow weir. On the right is another lake, which once provided power for the mill below. The valley soon becomes a little wider and the canal takes a dominant line towards the centre of the valley floor. We quickly pass another capped lock, adjacent to the reservoir spillway. Here a footbridge takes a path over the canal which meanders down the valley to come alongside Clough Mill, with its tall chimney.

Beyond the mill, the canal takes a more leisurely sweep through sloping fields, where the towpath here is lined by a strong dry stone wall. After some distance another capped lock is reached,

Entrance to the Standedge Tunnel. A few years ago, someone asked the British Waterways Board for permission to swim the full length of the tunnel. He was disappointed. The portcullis will no doubt deter other like-minded individuals, if such there be

and if we look back from this point we can appreciate the true grandeur of the Colne valley with the high moors of the Pennines all around.

Just before this lock is a wide turning basin, and below it the canal slowly winds its way through sloping fields on either bank, until further along to the right another mill dominates the valley floor. Soon another capped lock lowers the canal beneath a neat bridge, and after a short distance yet another capped lock is reached at Waring Bottom.

Our walk continues forward down the valley, and after a while we pass two filled-in locks, almost overgrown with the trees, but the towpath is surprisingly wide and clear and is well used. At the second lock a roving bridge spans the tail end. Ahead, the canal passes along through a wooded area on the left-hand valley side. At this point the canal and river are at roughly the same level and the towpath acts as a causeway in between. Relatively large trees grow from the towpath edge. After a while a mill leat parallels the canal, while the main river veers off to the right. We soon reach another lock, beyond which a mill building dominates the valley floor to the right. A wooden footbridge crosses this lock chamber and leads to a picnic area in Shaw Carr Wood beyond. Below the lock, the towpath is banked on the right and a mill leat alongside carries water to the mill. The woodlands continue along the left bank of the canal. Soon a large-diameter pipe parallels the towpath side, partly overgrown. As we near the mill, on the right, its tall chimney towers up on the skyline. Way down the valley ahead, the clock tower of Slaithwaite church can just be seen.

The lock adjacent to the mill is also capped. On both the right and left sides of the valley stone terraced houses survey the scene below. On the right, we pass the imposing buildings of Upper Mill, our path crossing over the access road. Ahead is another mill, and its tall chimney stands high above the valley floor, while up on the left the now parallel railway runs across a tall viaduct. A paved road substitutes for the towpath along this section, offering access to Upper Mill. Ahead another lock is capped over; on this occasion, a picnic area has been imaginatively laid out over the lock chamber, and trees planted on either side. Below the lock the canal line is completely filled-in, yet a small hump-back bridge still carries a path over the old canal line into a car park on the left, created out of an old wharf area. This bridge has deep wheel tracks worn in the stone.

Now we are almost in the centre of Slaithwaite, a town that has turned its back on the canal. Ahead, a 700-yard section of canal has been filled in, right through the town centre. Part has been used to create an attractive garden, though elsewhere a bus park blocks the route, which makes a sad ending to our exploration of this unique trans-Pennine canal.

Further reading

C. Hadfield and G. Biddle, *Canals of North West England, Volume 2*. David and Charles, 1970.

'The Huddersfield Canals' – Towpath Guide, Huddersfield Canal Society.

6 Wales

The Llangollen Canal

from Chirk Aqueduct (SJ 286373) past Froncysyllte and
Trevor to Llangollen Wharf (SJ 196433)
Maps 117, 125 and 126

PRECEDING PAGE *The Monmouthshire and Brecon Canal, Bridge No. 162*

The idea of developing a series of interconnected canals as part of a general scheme was prevalent in the 'Canal Age'. All too often these grandiose master plans failed through lack of finance, and as a result the proprietors had to make the best possible use of what they were able to achieve. The Llangollen Canal, or Shropshire Union (Welsh Branch) as it later became known, falls into this category. The original scheme was promoted by industrialists from around Ellesmere and Ruabon, who formed the Ellesmere Canal Company. They planned a canal linking the Mersey and the Dee estuary with the Severn, starting at a new wharf at Netherpool (Ellesmere Port), and ending at a riverside dock in Shrewsbury, connecting with their works *en route*. Although an Act was passed in 1793 to enable this to be achieved, when the canal network was finally opened in 1805 it was far from complete. A section between Chester and Ellesmere Port was finished in 1795; while the central section of the main line only went from Trevor, through Chirk and Ellesmere, to Hurleston, where it linked with the Chester Canal. A branch went as far as Weston Lullingfields, near the Shrewsbury road, far short of its original destination. Llangollen Wharf was added as an afterthought when a navigable feeder was opened between Trevor and Llantisilio in 1808.

The Llangollen Canal was never a complete success, although it did prosper for a while, and in 1845–46 was absorbed into the transport network operated by the Shropshire Union Railway and Canal Company. Commercial traffic finally ceased in the early 1930s, and in 1944 the entire Llangollen Canal was officially abandoned as a navigation, by Act of Parliament. Fortunately the value of the water collected from the River Dee at Horseshoe Falls ensured that the channel was retained as a water supply duct. But all was not lost, and the publication of a book called *Narrow Boat*, in which Tom Rolt recorded a voyage around the English canals, combined with the efforts of the Inland Waterways Association, formed in 1946, possibilities emerged for using the canal as a pleasure cruising route. Some of the first hire boat bases were opened in this area, and as a result of public support the whole canal was officially reactivated as a navigable waterway; this status was formally confirmed in 1968, when the whole Llangollen Canal was designated a 'Cruiseway' under the Transport Act. Today, quite rightly, the Llangollen is one of the most popular inland cruising routes.

Our walk embraces the best of the canal and starts at Chirk Aqueduct, which bridges the border between England and Wales. The aqueduct is a masterpiece of design, with its ten masonry arches supporting and embracing a cast-iron trough which is carried high over the wide valley of the River Ceiriog. The structure, designed by Telford, was opened in 1801 and is 696 feet long. It is best approached along the B4500 road from Chirk, although by far the best view is obtained from near the Bridge Inn on the A5, in the valley below. Parallel is a slightly taller railway viaduct, built some forty-five years later.

Almost as soon as the canal has crossed the aqueduct it enters Chirk tunnel, some 459 yards long, with a wide railed towpath throughout. The tunnel is straight but the towpath in the tunnel is very uneven in places and the railings are rusted, which makes it sensible to take a torch, though often the lights of passing boats can guide the way. On leaving the tunnel, the canal enters a long, deeply wooded cutting. A sloping pathway joins the towpath from the right near the tunnel mouth and offers access to Chirk Station and to the road leading to the impressive and ornate wrought-iron gates of Chirk Castle.

The towpath through the cutting is wide and smooth. After the long straight reach, the cutting slowly curves to the right and ends when the canal bends slightly left, to run parallel with the railway line. On the left, the former parkland of Chirk Castle joins the canal bank. Once we are beyond a winding hole on the left, Chirk Castle can be seen in the distance on the brow of the hill, partly hidden between trees.

The towpath segregates the canal from a railway embankment for a short time, but after a while a line of trees between the railway and the canal provides a more pleasant walk, with bushes covering the banks on the left. Meadows filled with grazing cattle divide the canal from the railway on the right.

Ahead and slightly to the right we can see woods, with old quarry or mine workings partly hidden from view. The canal

The Chirk Aqueduct and its big but younger brother

again enters a cutting, leading to the mouth of the short Whitehouses Tunnel. The towpath extends through the straight tunnel, like that at Chirk, and similar precautions apply.

Beyond the tunnel the canal enters an attractive and peaceful wooded cutting, but it soon gives way to a wooded embankment, crossing a valley, with the railway on its own embankment to the right. After the attractive greystone Whitehouse Bridge, the canal escapes into another wooded cutting. Both canal edges are lined with huge square-cut stones, each with lifting holes. Tall trees soon offer welcome shade as the canal curves along to reach the strong arch of Irish Bridge, which carries the Ruabon road over the canal. A steep pathway links to the towpath before the bridge.

Just beyond the bridge, the canal enters the Dee valley, curving sharply to the left to take up a contour path clinging to the valley side. The Offa's Dyke long-distance path joins the towpath at this point, which enlarges for a while to become a track on the right bank of the canal. Below, a wooded hillside tumbles down to the banks of the River Dee. Through a gap in the trees, to the right, the impressive Newbridge railway viaduct, which spans the wide valley of the Dee at this point, can be seen. On the left bank the steeply wooded valley side falls abruptly down to the canal, which has been carefully carved to run along its own ledge. For the while mature trees obstruct the view over the Dee valley, but soon gaps begin to offer glimpses of Ruabon on the hillside beyond. After a while the track leaves the towpath and descends to the valley floor. The towpath continues forward, slightly muddy in places, protected by trees that line the right-hand bank. After a while it is possible to glimpse the Pontcysyllte Aqueduct as it crosses the valley of the Dee.

The towpath becomes wide and clear. On the left bank a battery of decaying kilns and other buildings surround a derelict wharf. Further along, the lower level of the Pen-y-Craig quarry, now overgrown, can also be seen. Limestone from it was, until 1954, transported to the kilns to be burnt; the bulk of this lime was used either in blast furnaces for fluxing, or for making tarmacadam. To the right we can glimpse the Pontcysyllte Aqueduct. Far beyond is a high peak capped with the ruins of Castell Dinas Bran. We are now on the outskirts of the village of Froncysyllte. The towpath along this reach is a very popular walk, as visitors use it to enjoy the view.

Ahead is an impressive lifting bridge which takes a road across the canal. The official route of the Offa's Dyke path leaves the towpath here to link with the nearby B5434 road, which subsequently crosses the valley floor. Many walkers, however, prefer to take the official alternative route, which follows the towpath over the aqueduct itself, ultimately linking with the main route at Trevor. Because the lift bridge is raised so often, pedestrians have been provided with their own high-level footbridge at this point.

After passing the narrows of the lifting bridge, the canal swings through 90 degrees to continue northwards. On the opposite bank a small wharf with lengthsmen's cottages and a workshop offers an attractive backdrop to the canal, which now begins to run along a straight and heavily wooded embankment that strides out across the valley floor. The wide towpath to the right of the canal is a popular walk.

The slim orderly form of the Pontcysyllte Aqueduct is in direct contrast to that at Chirk. The former is a massive stone structure, with the canal in an iron trough completely surrounded by extensive masonry supports. At Pontcysyllte a revolutionary construction technique was employed, with a totally cast-iron structure as the sole trough of the aqueduct. The trough itself, formed into nineteen arches, was then laid along the top of eighteen slender masonry piers, each hollow towards the top to save weight. The whole magnificent structure, designed by Telford and Jessop, is 1,007 feet long and carries the canal 120 feet above the River Dee. The work took ten years to complete, and when the aqueduct was opened in 1805 it had cost over £47,000 to build. To maximize the water cross-section, the towpath is cantilevered over the top of the trough. Pedestrians and horses are given the protection of a handrail, but the boats only have some 12 inches of metal above the waterline, on the left-hand edge, to shield them from the dramatic drop below.

Walking across the aqueduct is an exhilarating experience. The wind whistles through the railings and the views down are quite remarkable. Looking to the west, we can see a medieval stone-arched road bridge as it crosses the river far below.

At the far end of the aqueduct a neat cast sign, in both English and Welsh, recounts its statistics. Just beyond, a footpath offers a good view of the piers and the delicate iron arches that give the aqueduct its strength. For the energetic, this path can be followed

Trespasser's-eye-view of the Pontcysyllte Aqueduct, from the south bank of the Dee

Water over water; the Dee from the Pontcysyllte Aqueduct

as it continues down to the river's edge, where it offers the walker another unusual view of this impressive 180-year-old structure.

Once across the aqueduct, the canal enters Trevor Wharf. The towpath continues along over a wooden swing bridge, which crosses the entrance to two side docks. Ahead, a white-painted bridge crosses to the main wharf. We will ultimately follow that route, but before doing so it is worth continuing forward to the solid stone bridge at the far end of the wharf. By passing under the towpath arch of this bridge, we can see the extensive but now overgrown double-pronged dock which was originally intended as the beginning of the Ruabon to Chester arm of the canal.

We return to the white bridge and cross to the neat main wharf, lined with hire boats. At the southern end of this wharf area the navigable feeder to Llangollen disappears under a low girder bridge. As there is no towpath for the first 50 yards we have to leave the wharf by the gate and cross the adjacent road, following a footpath alongside a housing estate. Soon a wooden footbridge crosses the canal, which we cross and turn under, and from here the towpath follows the left bank of the canal all the way through to Llangollen Wharf. After a while the towpath rejoins the official route of the Offa's Dyke path until the next footbridge. The canal route is an engineering triumph, closely following a contour high along the valley side. The whole path of the canal is now wooded and creates a peaceful, sheltered walkway. After a while the woods on the left cease and the towpath offers spectacular views over the valley floor, as the canal continues along its high, narrow, winding course.

Soon the canal curves to the right, and after two bridges the canal walls and bed are lined throughout with thick new white reinforced concrete. In 1982 a whole section of the canal in this area was breached when part of the bank slipped down to the Dee below. Consequently it had to be completely rebuilt at a cost of £500,000. Now the whole new section through to Bryn-Howell provides a stark contrast to the previous rustic section, yet the wide concrete edging makes an ideal walking surface. Although the next half-mile or so has been completely rebuilt, it does not detract from the overall beauty of the canal as it passes under the various brick and stone arched bridges following its course along the wooded valley side.

Just beyond Bryn-Howell Bridge lies the derelict concrete span of the former Ruabon to Barmouth railway line, the track of which has long since been removed. Soon after this point the canal is joined by the Trevor to Llangollen road (A539) which runs parallel to it, close to the right bank, for nearly a mile. Looking ahead and upwards we get a perfect view of Castell

Dinas Bran, a 1,062-foot-high peak, with its ruined castle keeping guard over the canal. The whole horizon of the valley side, high above the right of the canal, is a long rocky outcrop, foreboding and gaunt. On the left, the derelict course of the railway line gradually drops down below the canal level.

Sun Trevor Bridge is reached. A sign by it invites boat crews and the weary walker to sample the beer garden of the Sun Trevor Hotel. Just beyond the bridge the canal is again concrete-lined, though this section has mellowed with the passage of time. A local in the pub told me that this was the spot where in 1945 a breach in the canal bank had swamped a train on the line below, knocking the engine completely off the track and killing the driver. When the canal was repaired it was concrete-lined and doubly reinforced.

The canal now creeps along its own track, dives under a main road, and bends sharply to the left to avoid a stone cliff face ahead. Soon the main road that crosses the bridge drops down below the canal level on the left. The canal, on its contour route, winds off to the right through a pinewood. The towpath along this reach is very broad and rhododendron-lined. At the end of this reach the Llandyn stone bridge crosses the canal, and beyond this point the canal is at its most beautiful. On the right, mature trees protect the canal bank while sheep graze on the steeply sloping pastures beyond. Ahead a wooden lift bridge, in the upright position, creates a mirror image in the canal. Cattle also come down to the canal to drink the clear water. The whole scene is idyllic.

After the bridge, the course of the canal grows more rocky as the slope to the right becomes even more abrupt. The canal turns sharply to the right after a while and takes a very narrow profile on a ledge cut from the rock, over which trees make a canopy. The canal is so narrow along this reach that there is space for only one boat at a time. To the left, below the towpath, the bank drops almost vertically to the road below. Soon, through gaps in the trees to the left, we can see the outskirts of Llangollen. After a while the canal widens and is lined with moored boats as it comes out from under the trees to enter the town. The canal is high on the valley side above the town and a glance to the right, over the towpath wall, offers a fine view of the rooftops and beyond them the River Dee.

We soon reach Llangollen Wharf, where horse-drawn trip

At Trevor; the derelict dock which was once busy with boats carrying cargoes of coal and stone to the Pontcysyllte ironworks

boats ply for trade. The old wharf building has been tastefully converted into an award-winning Canal Exhibition Centre. From the wharf, standing high above the town, a steep lane goes down to the Bridge End Inn.

Narrow boats visiting Llangollen are only able to proceed about another 50 yards beyond the wharf, where there is a winding hole for them to turn. However, the towpath continues alongside the feeder all the way through to Horsehoe Falls. It is a beautiful forty-minute walk, each way, for those with the time to spare.

Just beyond the winding hole, high on the right bank, is the permanent site of the International Eisteddfod. Behind is the towering height of Castell Dinas Bran. For a short distance the canal line passes through the outskirts of Llangollen; it then passes beneath the A542 road before reaching Pentre Felin. The canal engineering then becomes more interesting as the feeder channel crosses a small stream on a very solid stone embankment with a small aqueduct, before entering a rocky cutting paralleled above by a side road; part of this length is bitumen-lined. Soon a white-painted chain footbridge crosses both the canal and the River Dee, by the Chain Bridge Hotel. Beyond this point the canal runs through a wooded area until it reaches the Valve House, built in 1947 to control the flow of water into the canal; the rate is fixed at six million gallons per day.

A path leads beyond the Valve House to Horseshoe Falls, a crescent-shaped weir designed by Telford to retain a constant supply of water to the canal. The Horseshoe Falls are an attractive spot, with fields tumbling down to the River Dee. Across the fields lies Llantysilio church, in an attractive wooded site, offering a peaceful setting for the end of the walk, one of the most spectacular routes into Wales.

Further reading

C. Hadfield, *The Canals of the West Midlands*. David and Charles, 1969.

L.T.C. Rolt, *Landscape with Canals*. Allan Lane, 1977.

Edward Wilson, *The Ellesmere and Llangollen Canal*. Phillimore, 1975.

The Monmouthshire and Brecon Canal

from Llangattock Wharf, near Crickhowell (SO 207178) via Llangynidr, Talybont, Penkelli and on to Brynich Lock (SO 079273)
Maps 160 and 161

Few canals can claim to owe their origin to tramways, yet many in South Wales were part and parcel of elaborate interchange networks with the aim of conveying bulk limestone, iron ore and coal from the quarries and mines to the valley works or the coast. The promoters of the canals saw the tramways as a key to a ready source of traffic which would expand as the demands of the Industrial Revolution increased. An Act of 1792 authorized the construction of the Monmouthshire Canal, and in the following year an Act for the Brecknock and Abergavenny Canal was passed. After much debate the promoters of the earlier Monmouthshire Canal persuaded those of the Brecknock Canal that the two canals should be linked to provide a through route along the Usk valley from Brecon to the coastal port at Newport.

Thomas Dadford was appointed engineer for both schemes, which were developed piecemeal as the tramway networks provided their traffic. As a result the Brecknock and Abergavenny Canal was not fully opened until 1812. Its character was defined very much by the mountainous setting which was responsible for its contour design. Unfortunately for the canal, the value of the local railway system was quickly established and by the 1850s plans were already afoot to replace the canal by more railway lines. Although the canal companies united and struggled for a while to retain their trade, they were finally taken over by the Great Western Railway Company in 1880, after which decline was inevitable. The tramways were closed and the last commercial traffic left Llangynidr Wharf in 1933. Fortunately the canal route was retained as a water supply line for commercial users in the Pontypool area and remained intact.

The development of the Brecon Beacons National Park in the 1960s provided hope for the canal. The amenity potential of this attractive water route, winding along the edge of the mountains, overhung with trees, offering spectacular views in sharp contrast to the tiny scale of its stone bridges and locks, made it extremely attractive for waterway-lovers. In 1968 the Monmouthshire and Brecknockshire County Councils reached an agreement with the British Waterways Board for the canal to be completely restored and maintained as a through navigation in its upper reaches. It was reopened in 1970 when a low fixed span at Talybont was replaced with a new lifting bridge and the Brynich Lock restored. Since then, the 33-mile-long canal has become one of South Wales's tourist attractions.

Our exploration covers the upper reaches from Llangattock, near Crickhowell, to Brynich Lock, just under 2 miles from Brecon. The A40 road, with its regular bus service, offers access at both points.

The choice of Llangattock as a starting point rests on its visual links with the industrial past. Behind ruined lime kilns, just north of the village above bridge No. 114, we can still trace the old tramway as it rises sharply to the limestone quarries in the hills beyond, above which is the new Craig-y-Cilau nature reserve. Access to the canal towpath at bridge No. 114 is gained in a novel way by using stone treads, sticking out from the downstream wall of the bridge, as a series of steps. Once on the towpath the extreme clarity of the water immediately takes the eye: few canals can claim to have water so clear that it is possible to see the bottom for the majority of their length.

Turning north under the bridge we can see the ruined and partly earth-covered arches of the old lime kilns situated on the opposite bank. About 100 yards further on is bridge No. 115, beyond which, on the left bank, is an old wharf now used as a private mooring. On this wharf are an extremely well-preserved battery of stone-built, ivy-covered lime kilns. A neat little cottage by the kilns reminds us that the lime burners used to live on site to keep the fires burning twenty-four hours a day.

Beyond the wharf the canal turns sharply to the right into a tree-lined reach. What is remarkable is that a stream passes directly under the canal at this point, deep down in a cutting below, and large trees grow from the embankment in between. Almost immediately the canal widens to provide a turning point for craft. Here, just beyond the towpath fence on the right, a small circular Great Western Railway Company boundary marker can be seen, mounted on an old length of railway line which is embedded in the steeply sloping bank that rapidly falls away from the canal. The next reach of canal, like much of the first part of the route, has been carefully carved from the valley side. As the towpath rounds a bend, some very impressive views can be enjoyed over Llangattock village and Crickhowell to the Black Mountains beyond. The canal parallels the River Usk, but high on the valley side meandering along a contour course. The towpath is wide and clear and well maintained, and initially offers an ideal walking route.

From bridge No. 118 to bridge No. 122 a whole section of the canal has been concrete-lined. The lining forms part of the protective work that has been necessary to keep this contour canal open, especially after a serious breach in 1975 near Llanfoist.

For the next 2 miles the towpath provides a scenic level walk, in part shaded by trees but frequently offering spectacular views of the valley below and the hills above. Unfortunately, after bridge No. 124 the towpath deteriorates and long grass and weeds obscure the way as far as bridge No. 128, with a short respite near bridge No. 125, where a cart track supplements the towpath to reach some old stables by the canal. After bridge No. 128 the towpath is again perfectly maintained and provides an adequate walking surface for the remainder of our route.

About a mile further on we reach the outskirts of the village of Llangynidr and the bottom lock of the group of five which lift the canal nearly 50 feet for much of its final course through to Brecon. A by-road runs parallel to the canal at this point. Adjacent to bridge No. 133 lies the Coach and Horses public house. Just above this bridge the canal takes a U-turn to cross over the deep valley of the River Crawnon on a curved stone aqueduct. It feels strange to look across the wooded valley, over the rooftops of the cottages below, and see boats moving almost at right-angles past the wharf area beyond, perched high on the steep hillside. The path now rounds the bend and, after crossing a curved aqueduct, reaches a neatly painted lock above which is an extremely attractive wharf area, now used as a maintenance depot by the British Waterways Board. The whole wharf area is contained by an attractive stone arch bridge, No. 134. Beyond this bridge the canal bends sharply and soon moves into a deeply wooded reach. Ahead we can see the steep slope of Tor-y-Foel, a high peak that rises up beyond the canal. Passing round another bend, we see a pretty, secluded flight of three locks in a leafy glade. The two top

Energy-saving route for narrow-boat people only: Ashford Tunnel

locks incorporate an interesting engineering feature: a side reservoir is linked to the pound between them, supplying water via a culvert underneath the towpath. By the top lock a cast-iron half-mile post ($32\frac{1}{2}$ miles from Newport) can be seen; a few of these posts, some broken, remain at various points along the canal, but this one seems to be the best preserved. Above the locks, around a bend, is a little picnic site and a little further on, before bridge No. 136, a set of white-painted stone cottages stands beside the left bank.

After another mile the valley starts to open out and a road rises from the valley floor to reach the canal. Here the canal enters a shallow cutting at the end of which is the minute Ashford Tunnel, 375 yards long, with no towpath. It is straight, and the other end can be seen easily. The stone-faced tunnel portal looks hardly large enough to allow a boat through. The towpath rises slowly over the portal to link with the road that passes over the top of the tunnel. At the other side, the canal parallels the road for about 100 yards before they part company, the canal taking up its straight contour course through a glade of trees for about a quarter of a mile. Just before the next bridge, No. 142, an old warehouse and stable building have been converted for residential use; below them is the Traveller's Rest public house. Beyond the bridge a row of lime kilns and a derelict wharf can be seen on the left bank; this wharf was once the terminus of the Bryn Oer tramway. Two huge pipes convey water from the Talybont reservoir over the canal near here, and a short distance further on is the disused bridge of the former Brecon and Merthyr railway.

The canal passes through most of the village of Talybont on an embankment. After crossing an aqueduct and rounding a bend we are confronted with a modern, electrically operated steel drawbridge, constructed in 1970 to replace a fixed span which previously blocked the canal.

After passing through a tree-lined cutting beyond the village, we find that the scene has changed completely: on both sides of the canal pastureland dominates and the canal takes on a rural appearance with functional wooden drawbridges contrasting with the stone bridges of the earlier length. After a while the canal makes a sharp bend into the village of Penkelli, where the grounds of the Royal Oak link with the towpath. Beyond bridge No. 154 the winding point has now been developed to provide a

Bridge No. 161, looking west

slipway with an adjacent parking place. Beyond lies Pencilli Court, an old farm complex with its own wooden-decked draw-bridge offering access to the fields beyond.

Leaving Penkelli, the canal follows a meandering path, at times on a small embankment, as it crosses fairly flat countryside on its way towards the River Usk. After a while the canal winds through a spinney and crosses a small aqueduct. This low stone structure has no towpath rail to offer protection from the brook a few feet below. Soon we find a tall, three-storey house on the left bank.

Beyond a bridge, the canal swings slowly round to link with the bank of the River Usk, which lies in a steeply wooded cutting some 40 feet below. After a while both part company, and the canal curves off through meadows. After bridge No. 161, we can enjoy some very good views of the Brecon Beacons by looking to the left, where the peak called Pen-y-Fan towers on the horizon. Soon the canal curves under bridge No. 162, where the towpath crosses to the left bank. From this bridge we can catch a glimpse of the low but massive stone four-arched Brynich Aqueduct as it strides across the rocky valley of the River Usk.

Once across the aqueduct the canal bends sharply to the left; ahead lies the neat Brynich Lock, preceded by an equally neat stone overbridge. At this point a by-road crosses the canal. The A40 road lies close by, offering access to buses for Brecon and Crickhowell.

The Brecon and Abergavenny Canal now forms an integral part of the Brecon Beacons National Park. It is the only canal completely within one of the national parks.

Further reading

I. D. J. and H. Jones, *The Brecon and Abergavenny Canal*; a short guide with maps compiled in 1983.

R. Alan Stevens, Towpath Guide No. 2 – 'Brecknock and Abergavenny and Monmouthshire Canals'. Goose and Son, 1974.

The Montgomery Canal

from Dolfor Lock (Newtown) (SO 137927) via Abermule and Garthmyl Bridge to Berriew Aqueduct and Berriew Lock (SJ 189007)
Map 136

The Montgomery Canal is one of the few able to claim royal patronage. The Prince of Wales' Committee has already co-ordinated the provision of funds for the restoration of $5\frac{1}{2}$ miles of the canal, between Buttington and Wern, and is now actively participating in the revival of further lengths. The Prince of Wales visits the canal regularly to see what progress has been made.

Merchants in Welshpool and Newtown were the original promoters of the canal. It was seen as an extension of the Ellesmere Canal Company's new branch at Llanymnech. The Montgomery Canal Company was formed in 1792 to construct a canal from Llanymnech to Newtown, with a branch to Guilsfield; it was built in two sections due to lack of money. The link from the Ellesmere Canal branch through to Garthmyl, a few miles beyond Welshpool, together with the Guilsfield arm, was completed in 1797. The second section, from Garthmyl to Newtown, was not opened fully until 1821, under the auspices of a new and separate Montgomery Canal (Western Branch) Company. The canal's main line is thus unique in that it was built and owned by two separate companies and relied on the branch of a third for access to the national network.

The main trade of the canal was the carriage of limestone, and vast banks of kilns were built at principal wharfs along the line. In its heyday Newtown Wharf had twenty-six kilns. Coal was also a major commodity, with numerous wharfs built to serve both villages and lime kilns, while timber was one of the main exports. Agricultural produce also created outward traffic and return general goods were stored at the various company warehouses.

By 1836 a fly-boat service had been introduced throughout the canal, offering a through service between Newtown and London. At this time the canal was profitable and trade was increasing; however the threat of railway competition caused the two Montgomery companies to join the Shropshire Union of Canals and

Railways by 1850. Fortunately railway plans were slow to evolve, and the canal survived as a viable enterprise until World War I. After that low levels of maintenance dissuaded trade and cheap lorries, surplus at the end of the war, soon competed with the railways to draw away the remaining traffic.

The end of trade came suddenly, on 6 February 1936, when a breach drained the canal near its junction with the Llangollen Canal. The LMS Railway Company, the then owners of the canal, decided that it would not be profitable to repair the breach and sought to abandon the waterway. Legal abandonment was finally achieved in 1944, by which time nature had taken its toll. Since then portions of the canal have been filled in, bridges lowered and the terminus of the canal at Newtown sold and put to other use.

The first prospect of reviving the canal came in 1967 when the Shropshire Union Canal Society was formed. Restoration work started at Welshpool in October 1969 where, after clearance of the canal, the first boat for thirty-five years was able to reach Welshpool Wharf.

In 1973 the Prince of Wales announced that his Committee, together with the Royal Variety Artists' Club of Great Britain, intended to promote the complete revival of a 7-mile stretch of canal between Ardleen and Welshpool. Since then restoration work has gone from strength to strength. Most recently people from the Community Task Force, sponsored by the Manpower Services Commission, have been undertaking general and tow-path improvements between Freestone Lock and Welshpool – a section of which is included in our walk. In June 1983 consultants produced a report which suggested that the whole canal should be revived for navigation at a cost of about £9 million. For the time being, however, walkers can enjoy the waterway, and our exploration sets out to cover the least-known length of the canal.

The walk nominally starts at Dolfor Lock, about 1½ miles east of Newtown, above which the canal has been filled in. However, for those who want to start at Newtown a pathway leads from the town, for part of its way along the line of the canal. In the late 1950s this upper section and basin area were filled in to facilitate provision of a new trunk sewer for Newtown. Subsequently a high flood protection embankment was built along the north bank of the Severn, around the former basin area, covering over the old lime kilns and obscuring a riverside lane. A footpath now extends along the crest of this embankment, from the new footbridge over the river near the town centre, and links to a stile across the old canal line at the outskirts of the town. The path then passes under an old canal footbridge and continues onwards along the old towpath past Llanllwchaiarn and the site of Rock Lock to the metal gates of the modern Newtown sewage works. An access road turning southwards off the B4568, by Llanllwchaiarn church, also brings us to this point.

Our walk takes us eastwards across the field opposite, along the left of the tall hedge which now protects the Newtown 'Reclamation' Works. A level section of the field covers the remains of the canal line, which only becomes evident after about 100 yards among a group of bushes that now surround the remains of Dolfor Lock chamber. A small lockkeeper's hut is hidden under the branches on the left lock side. At the tail of the partly filled-in lock a neat red-brick overbridge spans the cut, beyond which is an overgrown wharf area with a former storehouse on the canal side, almost hidden by high weeds. In the field beyond, the profile of the dry canal bed can be seen. After about a quarter of a mile we reach a stile that takes the path over a fence and on to the right-hand side of Freestone Lock – an exciting place. The old metal rubbing bars at the entrance to the lock remain intact, but the lock side is overgrown, the old lock gates keeled over in the lock itself, while beyond the lock to the left, hidden in the mass of trees, is the lock cottage, which remains intact. A path comes down the hillside beyond and crosses the fine brick-arched bridge which spans the tail of the lock, using the ends of the lock wall to provide abutments. Just to the right of the tail of the lock, beyond the hedge, the River Severn sweeps nearly up to the canal bank. A feeder canal follows the riverbank here and supplies clear water into the canal below the lock. It is well worth following the feeder for about half a mile to its source at Penarth weir. This spectacular structure consists of two graceful curving weirs, one below the other, that cross the River Severn. An elaborate salmon ladder on the near side combines with three sluices, used for draining the dammed pool to allow repairs, to make the whole structure a credit to its designer, Josias Jessop.

Our walk continues eastwards from Freestone Lock, along the right-hand bank where the well-used towpath is separated from the river by a neatly trimmed hedge. Various holes in this hedge

RIGHT *The dead canal: to the east of Dolfor Lock . .*

OPPOSITE . . . *And the living: restoration of the by-weir at Newhouse Lock (top); cleaning out the autumn leaves at Pool Quay Lock (bottom). (This is four miles north of Welshpool and not on the walk described.)*

provide fishermen with access to their chosen spots. The reed-lined canal runs along a ledge cut from the hill slope. The River Severn drops down rapidly along the valley floor beyond. As we walk along we pass spill weir channels going under the towpath, with rusted paddle gears still intact. The canal meanders along its peaceful course completely undisturbed, hugging the contour of the valley side.

After a while the canal circles to the left and a road bridge crosses the canal some way ahead on a metal girder span inscribed 'Brymbo 1862'. Steps link the towpath to the road, but we continue alongside the canal, which soon swings to the right to cross the pretty, triple-arched sandstone Aber-Bechan Aqueduct, which carries the canal over Bechan brook. Beyond the aqueduct a fixed low-level span carries a local road across the canal, which now reaches a wharf opposite. Here the left bank is well wooded and falls sharply down to the canal.

Our route continues along the right bank, which is well mown and provides a very attractive rural walk. The Severn soon swings alongside the canal, and through the towpath hedge we can hear the river as it passes over a weir. The canal flows along its man-made ledge, cut from the valley side. In places rock outcrops, carefully blasted away, are visible along this reach. The canal is deep and clear, although reedy at the edge. After a while the River Severn moves off across the valley floor, while the canal remains following its wooded path. The canal widens at a winding point, and then continues on its meandering course towards Newhouse Lock. Along this reach water irises and other wild flowers abound, as the towpath becomes more overgrown.

Beyond a farm bridge the canal is wide and clear through to Newhouse Lock, and the towpath is neatly trimmed and well used by anglers. Just before the lock, the canal is high above the valley floor. A brick wall lines the left bank – perhaps the remains of a former wharf, but now protecting the gardens of the houses which nestle between the woods and the lock side. Stop planks retain the water level above the lock. The lower gates are still there, looking battered and decayed; The date '13.2.93' is embossed on one of the metal strengthening plates. Below the lock a neat bridge crosses the canal, with the towpath continuing beyond it on the right. A wooded lane borders the canal to the left for a short while. Beyond the towpath hedge, the River Severn runs parallel to the canal for some way before curving off across the valley floor, soon to be crossed by the new concrete span of the Abermule bypass. The canal follows a path along the steep valley side. A clearing in the woods to the left provides room for some apple trees which were at one time the orchard of Byles Lock cottage that lies ahead. The lock itself has recently been fully restored. The only problems are the thick green bed of duckweed which covers the water in the lock, and the unrestored locks on either side. A tiny brick bridge spans the tail of the lock, but our path continues along the hedged right bank toward the new bypass road that spans the canal. Fortunately a square tunnel has been created for the waterway, but the walker has to cross the road above and join the towpath again at the bottom of a steep bank on the opposite side of the dual carriageway. Beyond the road crossing, the canal soon abuts the Severn again, but a small wooded outcrop of land quickly separates the two. To the left hedged pasture provides a barrier between the canal and the busy road which curves round to Brynderwen New Road

By Abermule

bridge with its dramatic white railings linking to those of the adjacent Severn Bridge. A new brick pillar now supports the canal bridge in between the towpath and the canal, but does not block our way.

Beyond these bridges huge piles of sand, salt and grit line the canal bank on the left in a council yard and ahead, on the left, a neat boarded Shropshire Union Railway and Canal Company warehouse still remains intact. The towpath between the bridge and the lock is popular locally. The lock ahead has recently been repaired, and stop planks retain the water level. Just beyond the lock, a brick-arched bridge offers an impressive view over the white-painted wharf house and cottage beyond, on the right.

At the far end of the wharf another well-restored bridge spans the canal, and by crossing it we regain the towpath on the right bank. Along the next reach of canal the towpath is wide. Ahead, the wooded hills tumble down towards the canal and we can appreciate the skills of the early engineers in selecting their route. Just beyond a spur of land, where the canal curves slightly to the left, we reach a carefully restored swing bridge. The canal is in first-class condition here, with the towpath hedge carefully trimmed.

We soon reach Gianhafran Bridge, an ornate structure for such a rural canal, dated 1889 and with its name cast in the black metal girder beam and now neatly picked out in fresh white paint. The towpath ducks under the bridge and beyond is an impressive view down the Severn Valley. On either side we can see tree-lined spur valleys linking to the main valley floor, where lush pasture intermingles with woodland. Beyond the bridge, the main road rises to cross a wooded spur while the canal continues its valleyside course and is soon also lined by a wooded bank. The site of the Old Pennant Dingle Wharf can just be traced to the left of the canal. From here, the canal follows a narrow man-made ledge, the towpath on the right embanked above the flood plain of the river valley, and the water meadows a little way below. After a while the main road rejoins the canal, but lies at the top of a steep bank reinforced with dry stone blocks, which detract from an otherwise pleasant view. A little further on, where the road has been widened, the canal has been given a concrete edge not in keeping with the surroundings.

The road soon comes down to canal level, although partly shielded by a hedge. Ahead another swing bridge, No. 142, not yet restored, takes a farm track over the canal. The canal continues to parallel the road for a couple of hundred yards, then suddenly swings left towards the main road and disappears into a culvert, one of the major hurdles which will face the restorationists. Our path crosses the main road diagonally, and then passes through a wooden gate to rejoin the canal side. The towpath continues on the right-hand bank. On the left bank fields beyond the canal also hide behind a thin row of trees which line the canal side. We pass a winding point, and not far ahead a grey arched bridge crosses the waterway. Beyond it, on the left, is a neat wharf building with a slated wall that protects it from the prevailing wind.

We soon pass another restored swing bridge over the canal. A little further along a high-level footbridge crosses the canal, with trailing plants hanging down like a green wall across the waterway. At canal level a substitute plank bridge with a rickety wooden rail offers an alternative route, which fortunately we do not have to cross. The towpath along this reach is a profusion of colour with masses of wild flowers.

After a while we come to Tan-y-Fron Bridge, a weathered brick arch. We pass under it, although a path leads up to the lane above, and continue along the towpath, where a small old lengthsman's store house stands at the canal side. A little way on the canal curves to the right, and another culvert takes it back under the main road. A low brick wall spans this culvert, bearing a date stone '1949'. Rejoining the towpath, we follow the canal as it moves off at right-angles to the road, heading across between the flat fields for a couple of hundred yards before swinging east into its own private valley. Beyond this bend the canal takes a straighter course for about half a mile. The towpath quickly passes under a delightful brick-arched bridge, No. 135. Some way ahead, a neat farm lies alongside the canal by another bridge. We continue along the right bank of the canal, which after a while is temporarily blocked by a piped aqueduct.

The canal is now slightly embanked for a while and the towpath is wide and clear. Soon the canal curves to the left and then is confronted with another culvert, which goes under the Montgomery road, alongside which stands the large Nag's Head Hotel. Again a brick wall with a '1949' date stone indicates when the barrier across the canal was created. A gate takes us out to the roadside. Cottages and outbuildings opposite indicate where an old coal wharf used to be. Now the filled-in canal line serves as a lorry park, before it disappears into the trees. There is no way through, so our route turns left to cross the A483 in front of the hotel. At one time there were seven wharves operating here, with thirteen lime kilns in three separate banks. Trade in coal and limestone made the canal a thriving concern and brought custom to the Nag's Head.

Our route passes right of the hotel and follows a by-road to the north. A humpback bridge, No. 131, takes us over the canal, where access to the towpath is gained on the right through an entrance beside a green-painted cottage. The towpath along the next section is neatly trimmed, and the grass soft underfoot. We pass another bridge at the site of yet another old wharf, along a curving contour path, slightly above the fields and cottages on the right, past a spill weir and across some fields. After some distance a low-level pipe crosses the waterway, and ahead the houses of Efail-Fach lie either side of the canal.

We are soon clear of the village and later, to the left, a line of trees shields the canal from the fields beyond. Along this reach the canal is covered with water lilies which completely block it in places. The bracken by the towpath is almost as tall as the towpath hedge and obscures the view. After a while we reach a shaded glade of trees and soon the canal sweeps round to the right on an embankment to reach the Berriew Aqueduct, a very impressive structure over a deep wooded river valley. Lanes either side of the river pass under two flanking side arches. The main aqueduct has two wide spans which cross the river using a central pier; this pier rests on visible timber beams which offer a unique opportunity to see an example of this early civil engineering practice. The river bed itself is also carefully paved. Originally built of stone, the aqueduct was reclad with blue railway bricks in 1889, when a small plaque was added to the outside wall of the central span. The aqueduct was repaired in 1984 and has been re-opened.

Beyond the aqueduct as we look to the left the village of Berriew lies around the church, partly hidden by trees. Our walk continues along the canal embankment where, after some way, the canal curves to the right. We soon pass the point where a feeder from the Rhiw once fed the waterway. Ahead, the imposing structure of the Berriew Bridge spans the canal.

The next section of towpath is exceptionally well maintained.

A gently sloping ramp leads down from the road to join it, offering the only means of access to the lock cottage by the side of Berriew (Rectory) Lock. On the left bank a derelict wharf area now lies overgrown, while to the right a high hedge protects the towpath. We go through a white wooden gate to reach the lock – a splendid sight: the lock chamber has recently been completely restored, and new gates, built in 1982, stand ready for use. Beyond the lock we can see the canal stretching out along the valley floor leading towards Welshpool. Our walk ends here, and we return along the towpath to join the B4390 road. To the left is the A483 with access to Welshpool and Newtown, and to the right the picturesque village of Berriew.

Further reading

Sue Ball, *The Montgomery Canal: Its History and Restoration*. Shropshire Union Canal Society.

John Horsley Denton, Towpath Guide No. 4 – 'Montgomeryshire Canal and the Llanymynech Branch of the Ellesmere Canal'. Lapal Publications, 1984.

Stephen Hughes, *The Industrial Archaeology of the Montgomeryshire Canal*. Reprinted from *Montgomery Collections*, Vol. 69, 1981.

'About the Montgomery Canal'; six leaflets available from 2, Canal Yard, Welshpool.

Appendix 1

New Life for Old Canals?

Few people can understand why the canals became so neglected in the inter-war years. Yet looking back it is doubtful whether anyone then dreamed that the majority of the population, with so much more leisure time, would be able to benefit from them. If the truth be known, the canals were simply forgotten in the rush to create newer and faster transport routes. In the 1930s, however, a few people began to appreciate the idyllic life that these silent water-roads could offer. One of them was L.T.C. Rolt, who travelled the canals on a converted narrow boat and in 1944 published a delightful book called *Narrow Boat*. At a time of shortage during and after the war, the book offered its readers details of a hidden, mysterious world. A fellow writer, Eric de Maré, subsequently produced descriptions of the waterways themselves in *Canals of England* and suggested that they should be preserved as part of the national heritage. These two writers were joined by Robert Aickman, who used his literary talents to promote the canals in the journal of the Inland Waterways Association which he founded.

It is generally accepted that the narrow-gauge canals can never again become viable transport routes, but they can be put to good use. Storm drainage systems in towns rely on canals to divert peak flows, and in the countryside they are part of the natural drainage system. In fact, canals have been with us for so long that they are now an integral part of Britain. It is in this light that we need to consider their future.

A canal can, for instance, become a linear park. In some places, such as at Mile End in the East End of London, the local canal has been used as a focus for urban redevelopment. Instead of hiding the canal behind factory walls, the town planners in the London Borough of Tower Hamlets have cleared the slums and created a new park alongside the canal, which combines with the Canal Way walk to link with the larger open space of Victoria Park. The urban canal now provides a focus for local leisure pursuits.

In rural areas it may seem strange that people should need

additional leisure space. In prime farming areas, however, space is at a premium; few farmers relish trippers in their fields. So the idea of creating a country park along a rural canal is reasonable. Devon County Council, for example, have adapted the Grand Western Canal as a linear country park. The scheme has been running for nearly a decade and it is exciting to see how the concept has developed. Originally, the organizers set out to preserve one section of the canal in a 'natural', secluded state and to conserve aquatic life, but the passage of time has shown that an ordinarily maintained and used canal can offer a better environmental balance.

The real problem is simply what to do with the canals that have fallen derelict and have been officially abandoned as navigations. Fortunately, many voluntary groups around the country are currently active in trying to revive their local canals. The waterways restoration movement is over thirty years old, but it was not until 1960 that any tangible results became evident. In that year the National Trust, in conjunction with the Stratford-upon-Avon Canal Society, started their four-year task of rejuvenating the derelict 12 miles of the southern section of the Stratford-upon-Avon Canal. The achievement illustrated to people everywhere what could be achieved with proper coordination and planning.

The revival of this canal link led local enthusiasts to seek to reopen the long derelict Upper Avon Navigation, and so, together with the restored Lower Avon Navigation, recreate a cruising circuit that had been closed to through traffic in 1873. After the lengthy task of fund-raising and the problems of gaining a new Act of Parliament, the whole Avon Ring was reopened in 1974. Since that time other canals, including the Peak Forest and Ashton Canals, the Brecon and Abergavenny Canal, the Caldon Canal, and a 5-mile section of the Montgomery Canal, near Welshpool, have been revived.

To most enthusiasts, reviving canals means bringing them back to full navigation and linking them, where possible, to the existing navigable canal network. Canals were built to carry boats and act as transport routes and are best able to survive if fully restored. There is no doubt that the greatest attraction of a canal is to see a painted boat slowly chugging by, but the benefits of boats using the waterways do not end there. Every craft that uses a canal has to pay a toll or licence fee, which provides

Builders' and renovators' signs of passage, in the vicinity of the Foxton Flight

1910

1970

income to maintain the canal. In addition, the very movement of the boats keeps the channel clear, as the silt is washed out of the centre towards the banks while the action of the propeller chops the weeds which otherwise can rapidly block the canal. A live canal attracts attention from locals, which in itself will probably provoke interest in its future. Once the water in the canal is moving, it offers a haven for fish. Fishing is one of Britain's most popular sports and the fishermen using the towpaths help to keep them clear, thus making an easier route for the walker.

A realization that Britain's inland waterways were likely to be important sources of employment and tourist spending was identified in an Inland Waterways Amenity Advisory Council report (*Inland Waterways – Arteries for Employment and Spending*), published in 1980. The report concluded that people spent £55 million in 1979 to enjoy the 2,000-mile canal and river system controlled by the British Waterways Board. This spending in shops, local businesses and public houses supported over 14,000 jobs, many of them in rural areas.

A separate study based on the Llangollen Canal, conducted in 1980 by Joan and Tony Byrne of the Shropshire Union Canal Society, examined how much people spent on the 'canal side' during the holiday season. They found that some 10,214 voyages by canal craft were made along the canal, with an average of five people on board each boat. Using an expenditure figure of £30 per person per week, they calculated that the money generated by the holiday traffic on the Llangollen Canal alone was £1,532,100 in 1980. It was no small matter for the traders of Llangollen when their canal was closed by a breach for the whole of the 1982 tourist season.

An important argument for reviving derelict waterways is that they can create vital new jobs in otherwise deprived areas. The area around the Huddersfield Narrow Canal is a case in point. The local canal society produced a report on the job creation potential of the Huddersfield Narrow Canal as a navigable waterway, which suggested that, apart from several hundred short-term restoration jobs and valuable job training, once the canal was reopened two categories of permanent work would be sustained. First there would be canal-based jobs, servicing not only people in boats but also fishermen, walkers and other visitors, or 'gongoozlers' as the old working boatmen called them. Work would centre on boat hire, boatyards and boat-building, trip boats, restaurant and hotel boats, cafés, shops, pubs, garages and suppliers to these firms. Second, the actual running of the canal would generate full-time work. The report concluded that by reopening this one trans-Pennine canal, at least 310 extra full-time jobs could be created and as many as 450 or 500 people might find summer work.

Perhaps the most carefully developed case for the revival of a canal has been forwarded by Associated Canal Enterprises of Bath, in respect of the Kennet and Avon Canal. They based their arguments purely on investment and return, indicating ways of encouraging private-sector investment and creating regular spending within the canal's catchment zone. Their studies suggested that at 1979 prices, for the 45-mile length of canal within the Avon and Wiltshire county borders, over £1 million in private sector investment, £1 million in new local spending and 250 permanent jobs could be derived once the canal had become fully operational. Of course there would be costs: first, those of the actual restoration and the installation of basic equipment, and second those of the additional maintenance required by the restored canal, estimated at £2,500 per mile per annum. However, by 1983 the Kennet and Avon Canal Trust had raised over £800,000 from voluntary donations to finance the restoration work. Equally, the Manpower Services Commission, through its various job-creation efforts, was able to provide funds to meet the cost of labour for further work. The two local authorities would be required to invest some £1.2 million over a decade, but would be supported by the British Waterways Board. After much deliberation, and taking into consideration the potential benefits in terms of jobs, amenities and financial profits, the plans were given the go-ahead.

It is perhaps difficult to understand, with so much justification for restoration, why more is not being achieved. It seems to be a matter of priority. Although leisure time might be increasing quickly, with enforced leisure for the unemployed seemingly here to stay, the nation has to make the best use it can of a limited leisure budget. In these circumstances, with every organization clamouring for more funds for their own particular scheme, the battle of priority can be a great constraint. Ultimately, the final decision revolves around the ability to develop a wide base of public support. Those in power – councils, water authorities, even MPs – must be persuaded to think automatically of canals as part of the national heritage, a heritage that should be protected and developed for all to enjoy. Also, the general public must be shown how beneficial the restoration of canals can be.

Various canal societies have found that the development of small parts of towpath walkways has been a vital ingredient of progress. Clearing a through route along a formerly overgrown path, and carefully signposting it helps encourage local residents to visit it and to support a scheme to open the rest. This sort of project only requires two inputs – the goodwill of the owner of the canal and the physical effort of a few ardent enthusiasts with saws, axes and a means to dispose of the rubbish they accumulate.

It is interesting to look at some areas where progress has been made. An excellent example is that of the Basingstoke Canal, which lay neglected and overgrown until the Surrey and Hampshire Canal Society was formed in 1966. One of the Society's first tasks was to open the towpath as a series of walks and to produce a booklet, *Towpath Walks by the Basingstoke Canal*. It was first issued in 1970, and had already reached its third edition by 1974. Booklets about the canal's natural history and waterside inns later added new dimensions to the walks.

In much the same way the Stroudwater, Thames and Severn Canal Trust developed towpath walks along their canal. On the overgrown upper reaches between Chalford and Daneway they had to rebuild the path completely in places, and replace an overbridge across a lock where the original towpath route changed banks. The local landowner, the Bathurst Estates, contributed timber to facilitate the work; the result is one of the most idyllic canal walks anywhere. As one of its early aims the Droitwich Canals Trust set itself the task of reopening the towpath along the Droitwich Barge Canal. This has not only provided an ideal walk but has offered the focus for major fund-raising through sponsored walks, using the newly cleared route. The canal itself has been used to promote interest in and support for its own future.

Not all canal groups have been fortunate enough to obtain direct access to the whole of their chosen canal. An example is the Wey and Arun Canal Trust, which is seeking to restore 'London's lost route to the sea'. The canal was closed in 1871 and some sections were sold. In other places, adjoining landowners have developed their land, cutting off former access routes. Not to be deterred, the Trust has carefully plotted a continuous route along public rights of way, which enables much of the path of the former canal to be followed. The 36-mile route provides a linking pathway between the popular North Downs and South Downs Ways – passing through the Surrey hills, dense woodland in Sidney Wood, remote areas of the Weald and the lush water meadows of the Upper Arun, over outcrops of greensand and through wild marsh areas to reach the high chalklands of the South Downs. The Wey and Arun Trust have also used parts of their route for annual sponsored walks, which provide them with a substantial income to finance restoration work elsewhere on the waterway.

Old urban canals offer great potential for the development of valuable traffic-free walkways through the hearts of towns. A good example is the walkway developed by the Greater London Council. The idea is to revive derelict patches of land and provide a chain of small parks linked by a refurbished towpath, along the Grand Union Canal between Tower Hamlets in the east and Ealing in the west, where the canal now forms part of a separate project to create a Brent Valley Park.

The scheme began in 1966 when the GLC formed a London Canals Consultative Committee, with representatives from the GLC, the British Waterways Board and eleven canalside boroughs, to explore ways of developing the canal and its surroundings for leisure use. Part of the route was selected by the Central Electricity Generating Board to provide a line for a cross-London cable duct which subsequently offered a means of renovating the towpath surface. The first parts of the walkway, linking Little Venice to Camden Lock, were opened in the 1970s, as a result of the innovative action of the Westminster and Camden Councils. Subsequently a greater part of the 40-mile route, between Limehouse and Uxbridge, was named the Canal Way as part of the 1977 Silver Jubilee celebrations.

In 1978 the GLC approved the concept of Canal Way parks. To achieve quick results the original sites were on GLC-owned land, but other plots were then designated for development as fast as site clearance could proceed. By 1981 eight small parks had been laid out alongside the canal, with smaller-scale improvements at some twenty other places. Other existing parks and open spaces alongside the canal were altered so that they could face the waterside. More than £1 million has been invested in improving the visual amenity, of which £170,000 came from Urban Aid grants. The result is that some 15 acres of open space have been laid out, 3 miles of towpath improved and an additional 2 miles of towpath alongside the canal, between Victoria Park and Limehouse, opened to the public. The Council has demonstrated the value of the canal towpath as a traffic-free pedestrian route, offering a prime leisure facility in some of the most built-up areas of the metropolis.

Recently, a variety of urban canalside developments have been given awards in European Architectural Heritage Year, and have received Civic Trust Awards. Of special note are the extensive and beautiful warehouses of Gloucester Docks, being redeveloped as part of a wider conservation scheme, while the Cambrian Wharf redevelopment area and the associated James Brindley Walk in central Birmingham have set a style for similar developments elsewhere. Also, it is worth mentioning the forward-looking developments around Wigan Pier. Here the whole derelict canalside environment is being refurbished under a comprehensive inner-urban redevelopment scheme.

The British Waterways Board often advertise their canals as 'The Gentle Highway'; the name is fitting. The canals are a world apart. It is because of this that so many people today are willing to invest their time and personal effort in reviving the lost inland waterways. This is a far cry from the attitude prevailing immediately after World War II when the idea was just to 'fill them in'.

Whether you walk, sit, fish or boat, spare a thought for those who fight to protect the future of the canals, and especially for the Inland Waterways Association, without which there would be few canals to explore today. In the teeth of official apathy and neglect this entirely voluntary charitable group has campaigned and worked since 1946 to revive Britain's canal system. The national system is there now, with many once-derelict miles already back in use – but still more work remains to be done if future generations are to enjoy these Gentle Highways which provide a unique Back Door to Britain.

Appendix 2

The Potential of the Towing Paths for Cyclists

Gareth Lovett Jones

The main part of this book has dealt with the pleasures, and occasional difficulties, of walking on the towing paths. However, as a cycling enthusiast of a particular sort (the slow sort), and as a photographer whose bicycle was of great assistance in getting the pictures for this book, I felt that it was necessary to put the case for opening up this unique network of routes to people on bicycles. It seems to me that the potential benefits of such a transformation would extend not only to cyclists but to walkers of all kinds, and indeed to anglers, and might serve to stimulate increased public support and revenue for the beleaguered waterways.

All the bodies concerned seem to be generally agreed that the towing paths in themselves constitute an underused leisure resource of enormous potential – at least for ramblers and pedestrians. A succession of government-appointed committees from 1947 onwards made recommendations that some or all of the towing paths owned by the British Waterways Board should be officially designated as public rights of way. To date, this has happened to about one-third of the 2,000 miles of towing paths – with no coherent pattern since dedication has depended entirely on local initiatives – and in recent years management agreements with councils have become increasingly common. Until 1978, walkers were still in theory expected to obtain permits before using any of the towing paths remaining entirely under the Board's aegis.

Since 1974, Countryside Commission funding has been available for the improvement of towing paths as 'recreation paths', in other words as paths which do or might serve the needs of casual walkers, or people out for the day, as opposed to those engaged in longer-term activity on the long-distance paths. This meant that more consideration has been given to paths within easy reach of urban areas, of which canal towing paths are an obvious example. However, in 1983 an internal study was produced for the Commission which recommended the use of towing paths as long-distance routes. The question of who would be responsible for maintaining the routes, however, remains a problem.

The local authority view of the value of towing paths for walkers is generally also positive. In 1977 a study produced for the now defunct Water Space Amenity Commission, entitled *The Potential of Towpaths as Waterside Footpaths*, reported that twenty-six local authorites referred specifically in their structure plans to the recreational use of towing paths and many, particularly in urban areas, included proposals for future development. Special emphasis was placed on the importance of canals as 'linear open spaces'.

All this bodes reasonably well for those who travel on the soles of their shoes. Until very recently, however, positive pronouncements on the potential of the towing paths as cycle and pedestrian paths were very few and far between, nor did anyone think to commission a study on the subject. The Inland Waterways Association, for example, has no policy on the use of towing paths by cyclists. This is particularly sad in the light of the fact that the IWA's many campaign successes have chiefly been founded on its capacity for *drawing people in* to the separate world of the canals, and getting them involved.

The BWB's position on bicycles has always been markedly ambivalent. The WSAC report observed that, until the Transport Act of 1968, 'the traditional approach of the British Waterways Board towards the public use of their towpaths had been one of restriction', partly because of theoretical conflict between public access and the towing paths' role in canal maintenance, and partly because of 'the uncertainty surrounding the future of the waterways which made it difficult to do anything that would tend to establish rights of way'. Given the vicissitudes of the waterways' history since World War II, the failure of central government to allocate sufficient funds for basic maintenance and, until July 1979, the political threat which existed to BWB's independence, we may at least understand why unenforceable walkers' permits were kept in existence for years after the public had ceased to bother with them.

But this, of course, applied only to pedestrians. So far as cycling is concerned, I am sorry to report that there has recently been an all too evident move towards *increased* restriction. Until the end of 1982 all the prospective cyclists had to do was to send £1 to BWB headquarters in order to be issued with a year-long permit entitling him or her to take a bicycle on almost all the towing paths owned by the Board. No one could argue that this was not a good deal. However, the arrangement was never advertised: no attempt was made to sell the very pleasant idea of exploring the canals by bicycle to the public. Apart from word of mouth the Board relied entirely on the use of notice boards forbidding people to cycle on the towing paths *unless* they had permits – hardly an encouraging approach. It was only when the news spread, via press and radio, rather further than the Board had perhaps expected, that changes were felt to be necessary.

These came into force at the beginning of 1983, since when any application for a comprehensive permit has been answered with an application form to be completed and sent to the appropriate Area Engineer's office (there are seven of these). The applicant must now specify which canal or canals will be cycled along, approximately how often, and *why*. All applications are considered 'on their merits'. Access to the towing paths has thus been made far more difficult than it was under the previous arrangement, although the fee remains a nominal £1 per permit.

The reaction of the BWB to a growing demand for the use of its towing paths by cyclists has thus been anything but positive. Rather, it has withdrawn, snail-like, behind a rearrangement of the rules and regulations, without so much as considering the possibilities for increased public involvement and, with the right management, the increased revenue which this change might afford.

I am not convinced that the solution to this problem can lie in any kind of permit system. Certainly the permits in themselves will never be a significant source of funding. All they do is to damp cyclists' enthusiasm, until such time as the towing paths have been improved to accommodate them. One thing is certain, and that is that people riding bicycles – three million regular cyclists, four million who ride less than once a week, and five million children – are not going to require *fewer* facilities in the future.

The change in permit regulations slipped by without attracting attention from the media, but the same could not be said of the Board's decision in March 1983 to turn down a proposal from the Bristol-based cycling campaign organization Cyclebag to upgrade 10 miles of the towing path of the Kennet and Avon Canal between Bath and Trowbridge at a cost of £55,000, for use as a section in the longest segregated bike and pedestrian path yet created in Britain. Much of this 40-mile route is already open: a stretch running alongside the River Avon on the top of a dyke connects Avonmouth with Bristol, and between Bristol and Bath the route runs along disused railway lines. Negotiations on the Kennet and Avon towing path began in 1979, and the scheme has won the support of all the local authorities through whose areas it passes as well as that of local MPs, the Kennet and Avon Canal Trust (the body largely responsible for saving the waterway itself from dereliction), and the BWB's own Area Engineer's office at Gloucester. The arrangement proposed by the path-makers ensured that the BWB itself was not responsible for any part of this expenditure. The route could have provided a safe, level alternative to the murderously busy and in places hilly trunk road routes between Bath, Bradford-on-Avon and Trowbridge, giving people in villages along the Avon valley a direct cycling route into Bath city centre. But, despite all these factors in the scheme's favour, the BWB finally turned it down flat.

In the foreground, the murderously busy A36 south of Bathampton; in the background the alternative route for cyclists, the Kennet and Avon towing path, stands shamefully unused

A number of reasons were given by the Board for rejecting the plan. First is a foreseen conflict with other users of the towing path, in particular walkers, among whom the aged, the infirm and young children were specifically mentioned. Speaking as one who has walked this stretch of towing path on a summer Saturday, I can say that not very much of it is at present fit for use by the aged, the infirm or young children, and that except in the centre of Bath itself I saw very few walkers in these – or any other – category making use of the facility. One has also to remember that Cyclebag were proposing the construction of an entirely new, smooth path with an average width of six feet, at some distance from the water's edge, which would have been far more attractive to aged, infirm and very young walkers than the existing obstacle course. A path of such a width would surely be able to accommodate everyone.

Second, it was feared that the enjoyment of wildlife by other members of the public might be spoiled by cyclists. It is possible, I suppose, that occasionally a cyclist might disturb an amateur ornithologist by scaring birds away, but this would not be very common. Cyclists are no noisier than ramblers, and their mode of transport is virtually silent: wild creatures are very sensitive to footsteps, and I have often been able to get much closer to animals on two wheels than I would have done walking. Moreover it is generally walkers, not cyclists, who bring dogs with them.

There is another, related, area of concern here. Some conservationists fear that the creation of new paths could disturb valuable plant colonies already established on the canal sides. Clearly, sensitivity to what is already growing along the line of any bike path is necessary. But it is arguable that where many stretches of towing path are at present trodden into broad sloughs at difficult points, the engineering of a firm, clearly defined strip of cyclable and walkable pathway would 'contain' most travellers, so that more ground rather than less would be available for colonization by plants.

Then there is the already acknowledged potential for conflict between anglers and people taking boats along the canals, which was discussed in an IWAAC report of 1975, *Angling on the British Waterways Board System*. Nevertheless, at least in my observation of them, anglers and boat users seem to coexist quite amicably on the canals. The same is very likely to be true of anglers and cyclists, not least because many anglers arrive at

One of the reasons most frequently given for keeping 'cyclists' off the towpaths is that they will get in the way of 'anglers' . . .

the canal by bicycle! The BWB argues that anglers would have to be more careful when casting. Are they not already expected to be careful when walkers are going past? The amount of equipment around them was also cited as being incompatible with cycling. But in the first place the BWB's own by-laws state that no canal user, anglers included, should obstruct the towing path; and second, as already established, what was being discussed was a path set back from the water's edge which would in places create an improved waterside area on which anglers could spread their gear as they pleased without any danger of conflict.

The Board also feared that to create formal bike paths would be to encourage illicit use of the towing paths by motorcyclists and horse riders. Such people as are determined to use the towing paths already use them of course. But this problem could be overcome by careful design of stymie gates at all road access points, and the Cyclebag scheme suggested a design already found effective on the railway sections of the route. If such barriers had been put into use on others of the Board's towing paths (for example the Grand Union), the motorcyclist problem might already be much less pronounced. As far as horse riders are concerned, however, I am not convinced that they should be excluded from the widest towing path banks. The main problem is that the repeated passage of horses' hooves will quickly churn up all but a hard (and relatively costly) asphalt surface.

Finally, we come to the question of possible accidents between cyclists, or between cyclists and pedestrians, or anglers, or people stepping off their boats without looking first, or even the kind of accident in which someone inadvertently pedals into the canal. The Board sees cyclists as a potential threat to other users of the towing paths, as is shown by its recent decision to allow formal cycling routes on towing paths only when cyclists can be physically segregated from other users. But there is very little evidence to support this fear. The Board itself was unable to supply me with any examples of towing path accidents involving cyclists. Similarly, on the existing stretches of bike and pedestrian path between Bath and Bristol, and Bristol and Avonmouth, no accidents have been reported in the four years since the route opened, and the section between Bath and Bristol on the outskirts of Bristol has a recorded use of some 5,000 trips per week split roughly 50:50 between cyclists and pedestrians. On a length of the Cromford Canal in Derbyshire which is owned by the local authority and freely open to cyclists, there have been no reports of any accidents. On the new tarmac path running parallel with the Droitwich Canal, also officially open to cyclists, there have been no reports of any accidents. *Surveys of a Range of Cycleways* published by the Transport and Road Research Laboratory in 1982, showed no recorded accidents on ten of the fourteen routes surveyed, and only seven accidents spread between the remaining paths over a three-year period, of which exactly one involved a cyclist and a pedestrian.

It is important to grasp the nature of the design envisaged for the Kennet and Avon bike path. The illustrations are based on diagrams by John Grimshaw and Associates, the engineers for the proposed canal conversion, and the consultants to the Department of Transport who were responsible for a report entitled *Study of Disused Railways in England and Wales: Potential Cycle Routes* (HMSO, 1982), which suggested the use of certain canal towing paths as links in routes developed largely along disused railways. The first drawing illustrates the scene as canal explorers so often know it, with a narrow, muddy and pitted path dangerously, or at least inconveniently, close to the water's edge. The second shows the canal bank after upgrading, with a space of 5–6 feet between path and water for use by anglers, those mooring boats, or anyone wishing to sit next to the canal: this space would also act as a safety net for cyclists. The other drawings show workable variations where space is rather more limited.

Particularly important is the drawing dealing with the treatment of bridge holes. The poor visibility caused by right-angle bends at some bridges, coupled with the narrowing of the ground under the bridge, have been cited by the BWB as reasons to be anxious about cyclists (although in the Kennet and Avon scheme detours were to have been put in to avoid bridges entirely). But the rail barrier suggested here seems a perfectly adequate method of keeping all travellers on solid ground; it might be coupled with a requirement that cyclists should dismount and walk under the most difficult small bridges on the narrow canals. Where towing paths run through tunnels, the rail could be continued for the full length; some tunnels are already equipped in this way for the benefit of pedestrians.

Finally, where the towing path runs along a bank formation too narrow to accommodate path and greensward to the dimensions stated, there is often the possibility (at least in rural areas) of extending the formation a few feet outwards. This would of course be costly, and perhaps dependent on the demonstrable growth in popularity of routes already established. But the cost would still be minuscule in comparison to those involved in road engineering, and the waterways concerned would benefit from the strengthening of their banks.

There are in addition a number of inherently excellent reasons why formal bike and pedestrian paths should now be developed along canals. The first is that what the waterways need above all else is users. The canals still urgently need both money and volunteers to keep (or put) the water in them. It should not matter whether the public travel by narrow boat, on foot, or by bicycle: the more people who can move freely along the waterways, the more public interest in restoring them will be generated. How many people even in Birmingham itself know the Engine Arm Aqueduct, for example? Yet if the towing path beneath this

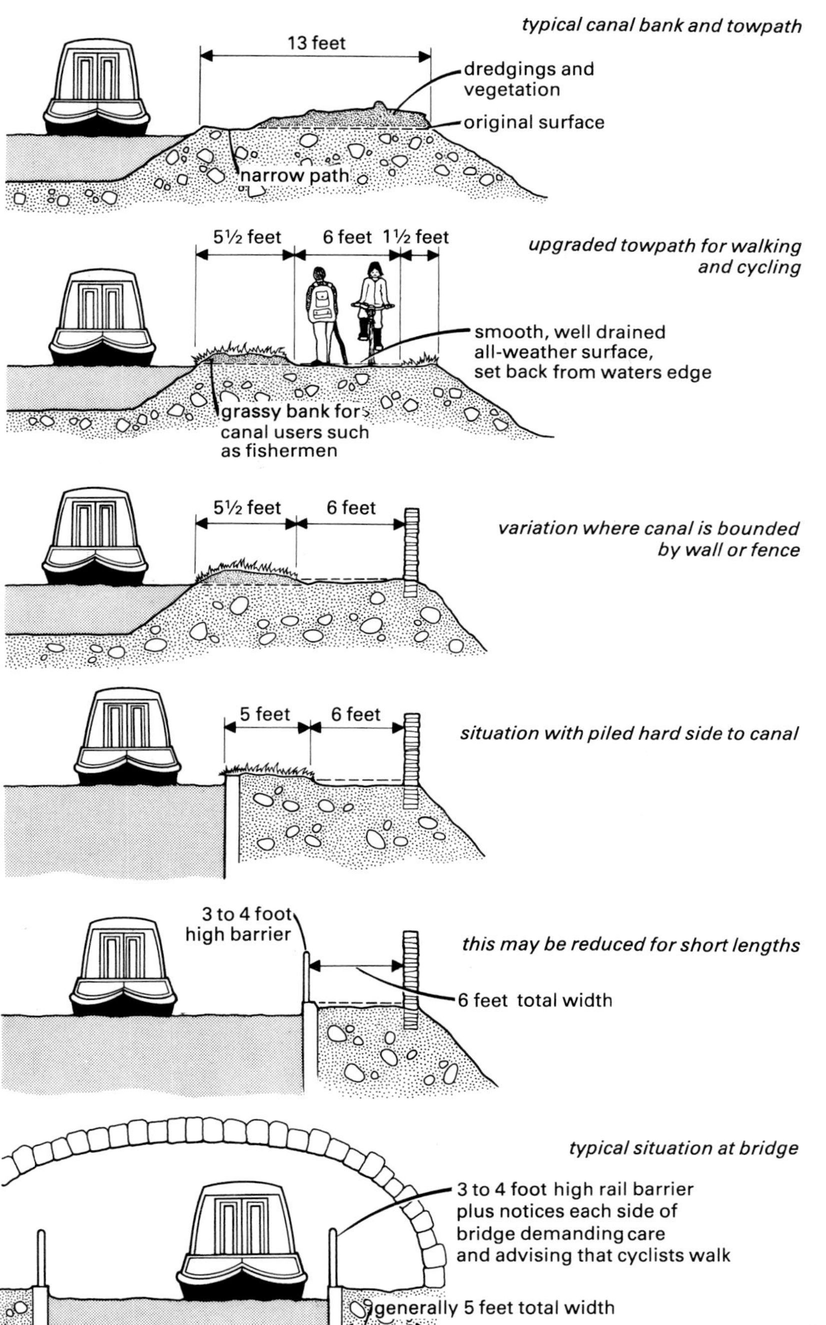

These drawings are based on diagrams by John Grimshaw and Associates

Ways of upgrading towing paths for shared use by pedestrians and cyclists

fabulous but dilapidated structure was a well-used cycling artery it would be quickly established as one of the landmarks of the city, and perhaps renovated. During the several hours which I spent in its vicinity I saw only one pedestrian, without even a dog to keep him company, on the towing paths there. The BWB simply cannot afford to chase people away.

There is an interesting similarity between the arrival of Cyclebag at the Kennet and Avon Canal, and the emergence of all those local voluntary groups who have helped save waterways since World War II. In both cases the official body, the BWB, has been presented with an independent outside force which cares about the amenity and has organized its own labour and resources. And in both cases, the amenity is improved for the benefit of *all* users. I think that this point is worth stressing. So many stretches of towing path are difficult going at present; yet it is the casual or less able-bodied walkers, rather than long-distance or mountaineering hikers, who should best be able to benefit from them. In the long term, upgrading of towing paths to a reliable standard would inevitably attract far more such walkers to the canals.

Many features of towing-path routes are specifically attractive to people using bicycles. They are level – particularly valuable when all nearby roads are hilly – and, most important of all, they are *segregated from routes carrying motor traffic*. The creation of formal bike paths along the canals as an alternative to busy roads would, without question, contribute towards a reduction in road accidents. As we have seen, the BWB fears accidents on canalside paths. But which is more likely to be serious – a collision between two cyclists on a quiet path separated from water by a distance of several feet, or one between a cyclist and a car or heavy goods vehicle on a busy road? All over the country, little-used towing paths could provide safe, quiet alternatives to dangerously busy roads for cyclists, for example allowing children to get to school. Children are one of the most important potential user groups for such paths, precisely because they are so vulnerable on the roads. The Department of Transport's publication *Road Accidents, Great Britain 1980* showed, in relation to distance travelled, much higher accident rates for children than for adult cyclists.

As was noted in a 1978 Countryside Commission working paper, *Cycling to the Countryside*, the towing paths make excellent 'escape routes' into the country from many urban areas including

London, Birmingham, Manchester and Liverpool. They also link urban centres, particularly in the Midlands and the northwest. Their redevelopment as bike paths could prove invaluable both to recreational cyclists living in towns who want a quiet way out, and to those who cycle from one town to another.

There are already a few very short lengths of canalside path in use as formal cycle routes. For example, there is the short section of the Cromford Canal, already mentioned, which links up with the High Peak Trail. A stretch of towing path in Newport, Gwent, is soon to be open to cyclists. There are also stretches of specially created bike path in Milton Keynes and Nottingham which, like the path at Droitwich, run alongside the canals on the side opposite to the towing paths! The *Study of Disused Railways* proposes links in its segregated railway routes along sections of towing paths on twelve canals, totalling some 25 miles in all. There is also, at the time of writing, a formal proposal from the Lea Valley Park Authority to use a section of the towing path on the Lea Valley Navigation as a bike path; this is being considered by the BWB. But the greatest single hope lies in the Cycle Tracks Act, recently approved by Parliament, which should make it much easier to open up those stretches of towing path already dedicated as public rights of way. However, such a law would not change much on the remaining two thirds of the network, at least until such time as the BWB rethinks its own position.

The notion of bike and pedestrian paths along the canals should be seen in a rather wider context. Since 1981, the government has been at pains to make known its increasingly favourable attitude towards cycling. The *Statement by the Secretary of State for Transport* on cycling policy of January 1982 was, effectively, the first policy document on the subject. Here it was announced that 'the Government very much welcomes the revived interest in cycling, which can bring benefits to the community in terms of reduced congestion, pollution and energy costs'. The *Statement* reported, among other things, on the appointment of cycling officers to each of the regional offices of the Department of Transport, on a programme of financial aid for innovatory cycle schemes which could then be monitored, on the conversion of some footways to shared use by cyclists and pedestrians, especially where this would get cyclists off dangerous roads, and on a number of studies being carried out at the Transport and Road

Research Laboratory on cycling accidents and possible remedial measures.

Except in certain new towns or large new housing developments where such facilities have been planned from the outset, the emergence of the shared bike and pedestrian path is a recent phenomenon. Such paths are marked by a blue and white sign showing a bicycle on one side, and pedestrians on the other, and they are appearing in urban areas wherever local authorities have the will to establish the routes. More often than not these are being made out of existing facilities, through parks or on other public ground, which have not had a very high level of use by pedestrians alone. Good examples are already to be found, for example, in London, Cambridge, Bedford, Nottingham, York and Middlesbrough.

We are, then, at a point in time when the Department of Transport has consolidated its views on the advisability of encouraging cycling and improving facilities to this end, and where some if not all local authorities are beginning to take practical steps on the ground. As this book goes to press, the Department is involved in discussions with the BWB which *may* serve to produce a number of pilot schemes along towing paths that can subsequently be monitored. However, it is the Department of the Environment which holds the BWB's purse strings, not the Department of Transport, and unaccountably the former has no vigorous policy on cycling. A change of chairman at the BWB has just been made, and it is possible that a new leadership may result in a more forward-thinking response to the cycling issue. In the meantime I can report that the Board has agreed to 'towing-path improvements' on the section of the Kennet and Avon canal between Bath and Bathampton, which means that at least those cyclists who have permits will be able to enjoy a smooth ride along this stretch – a very small step, but a step in the right direction.

In *Railway Walks* (1980) I put forward the notion of a network of segregated 'greenways' made for the benefit of cyclists, walkers and horse riders out of the 8,000-plus miles of disused railway tracks in England and Wales. To date, between 500 and 600 miles of such conversions have been opened to the public, but they exist almost entirely on truncated lengths of line converted locally in a random manner by the councils concerned, wherever railway land came into their hands and the money was available.

Local fishermen, seen next to the unused cargo boat inlet at the back of the Kellogg's factory, on the Bridgewater Canal

Had anyone thought seriously about the problem back in the 1960s, when this huge accumulation of potential routes was released, we might now have a solid network of railway 'greenways'. No one with any power did think about it, however, and even when some energy was applied to the problem in a Countryside Commission report of 1969, nothing cohesive was done. All efforts to establish interlinked bike paths on disused railways today are therefore incalculably more difficult than they would have been twenty years ago, since the routes have been broken up into fragments.

Thanks to the efforts of individuals and groups and, eventually, to government involvement, nothing like this has happened to those other redundant transit routes, the canals. Even when the line of a waterway is blocked through dereliction the land remains in public hands, and the only practical obstacles to reopening are financial ones. Furthermore, even where the waterway is a mass of mud or reeds, the towing path is usually there in some form or another. A network of greenways, bike paths or shared-use paths – call them what you will – could still readily be brought into existence along the 2,000 miles of canal towing paths.

For the present, for obvious reasons, the emphasis is likely to remain on the localized use of specific stretches of towing path where it can be clearly shown that these provide the only alternatives to dangerous roads. But this should not obscure the fact that an infinitely larger potential remains unrealized. Like roads, the towing paths are both a local and a national resource; their comprehensive upgrading would give us a national network of waterside bike paths similar in function to the motorway network, simultaneously a network of long-distance paths for hikers wanting to stay on the level and a series of 'recreation' paths for walkers in each urban area they traverse. The people using them would range from those exploring the country by way of the canals, through those exploring the canals *per se* (and both groups could include foreign tourists if the idea was advertised), to individuals travelling to and from work, or school, the shops, or visiting friends.

No one has yet made any estimates of the possible benefits to the economy of such a network of routes. Such a calculation would have to include not only increased spending on canalside facilities resulting from the growth in the number of travellers, but also savings on petrol and on highway and car repair costs. A great benefit would be the transformation of a certain number of commuting motorists into cyclists, encouraged by the safety and pleasantness of the new paths into leaving their cars at home.

On this comprehensive scale there is one other planning possibility which has relevance to the re-use of the towing paths. The 1980 IWA report *Waterways Survival?* included a recommendation that 'the waterways system should be considered as a linear *national park*, 2,000 miles long'. We have already seen how certain sections of canal have been successfully redeveloped into linear parks in both town and country. But the great advantage of establishing the waterways in their entirety as a national park is that their status as a recreational resource before all else would be formally established. The redevelopment of the towing paths for shared recreational use could then be explored in all its facets, bearing in mind that such redevelopment would inevitably have a solid, everyday, functional usefulness as well.

Appendix 3

The British Waterways Board is responsible for some 2,000 miles of canals and river navigations. Their small publication 'A Walk on the Wild Side' gives details of several pamphlets, also published by them, that describe the canalside walks throughout England, Wales and Scotland. Both 'A Walk on the Wild Side' and more extensive information are available from the Press and Publicity Office, British Waterways Board, Melbury House, Melbury Terrace, London NW1 6JX, telephone 01 262 6711. Prices on request.

Glossary

AQUEDUCT A bridge which carries a waterway over a road, railway or valley.
BASIN A wider area at the side or end of a waterway where boats can moor and unload.
CUT The name often given to a canal because it was cut from the ground.
DREDGER A machine, either land- or water-based, to scoop mud and rubbish from the waterways.
FLASH LOCK OR STAUNCH One of the earliest methods of overcoming a change of level on a navigation. It consisted of a single removable barrier across the navigation channel. When it was opened a flash of water was released from the higher to the lower level to permit through navigation.
GONGOOZLER Someone who stands idly about on the canal side watching what is taking place.
HIRE BOATS Pleasure craft offered for rental by firms for holiday cruising.
HOTEL BOATS Pleasure craft with small cabins in which people stay on board as in a hotel.
JUNCTION A place where one waterway links to another.
LEGGING The way in which boats were propelled through tunnels without towpaths before they had engines. Men lay out sideways on planks and 'walked' their feet along the tunnel sides.
LENGTHSMAN A waterways employee whose job it is to maintain a section of the canal.
MERSEY FLAT A type of sailing barge that once carried the bulk of traffic on the River Mersey and on neighbouring canals.
MOOR To tie up a boat at the waterside.
PADDLE The name given to the small sluices which allow water in and out of lock chambers.
PADDLE GEAR The machinery used for opening and closing paddles.
POUND A stretch of water between locks.

PUDDLE The special clay mixture which lines the beds of canals to keep them watertight.

RESERVOIR The source of water for a canal, usually formed by diverting or damming a stream.

ROVING BRIDGE (TURNOVER BRIDGE) A bridge where the towpath crosses from one side of the canal to the other. Often it is curved in a special way so that the towrope does not need to be unfastened when the horse crosses over.

SIDE-POND A small pond at the side of certain locks, used to save water during lockage.

SILL (CILL) The solid ledge against which the bottom edges of lock gates close.

STAIRCASE Locks which are so close together that there are no pounds between them.

STOP PLANKS Lengths of wood that can be placed across the canal in specially constructed stop-plank grooves to make a dam. They are used to retain water in one section of canal while the next section is drained. Also for safety purposes stop planks can be quickly inserted to prevent a major flood if the canal is breached.

SUMMIT LEVEL The highest level of a canal. Also the level at which the main water supply is required.

TOWPATH (OR TOWING PATH) The path built alongside canals and navigations for the towing horses to walk along. In places these are called hauling ways.

WEIR An overflow arrangement to take away surplus water safely, while retaining a navigable depth.

WINDING HOLE A wide place where boats can be turned.

Index

Page numbers in *italic* refer to illustrations